MW00930515

Caw of the Wild

Caw of the Wild

✦

Observations from the Secret World of Crows

Barb Kirpluk

iUniverse, Inc.
New York Lincoln Shanghai

Caw of the Wild
Observations from the Secret World of Crows

Copyright © 2005 by Barb Kirpluk

All rights reserved. No part of this book may be used or reproduced by any means, graphic, electronic, or mechanical, including photocopying, recording, taping or by any information storage retrieval system without the written permission of the publisher except in the case of brief quotations embodied in critical articles and reviews.

iUniverse books may be ordered through booksellers or by contacting:

iUniverse
2021 Pine Lake Road, Suite 100
Lincoln, NE 68512
www.iuniverse.com
1-800-Authors (1-800-288-4677)

Names of some characters have been changed to protect their privacy. While the situations depicted here are true, some characters have been amalgamated and fictionalized for the sake of clarity. Resemblance to real persons, therefore, is coincidental, and not intentional.

ISBN-13: 978-0-595-36268-4 (pbk)
ISBN-13: 978-0-595-80713-0 (ebk)
ISBN-10: 0-595-36268-0 (pbk)
ISBN-10: 0-595-80713-5 (ebk)

Printed in the United States of America

For my grandmother. The memory of her beloved canaries, held gently in hand, inspired my own love of birds. And for all the crows whose lives have touched mine.

Contents

Part III   Summer 2002

Acknowledgments

I'd like to thank all the kind folks who listened to my rambling tales of crows, collected articles about them, wrote me notes, drew maps on little scraps of papers, or typed out elaborate anecdotes of crow sightings—including the story of the beer-swilling derelict crows on one dog-walker's route. You helped me find roosts and kept ears and eyes out for crows when you had previously not given them a second look. You were even moved by my evangelistic fervor to give crows a chance when you had previously hated them. You gave me crow medical advice, looked through my pictures of the remarkably similar characters, and scoured Internet mailing lists for anything pertaining to my beloved black birds. The list below is selective rather than inclusive, but thanks as well to all who helped along the way: Carmen, Mugs, Steve F. and Suzanne F., Buntin, Caryn, and Peter, R. Hospers, Fran, Judi, Carole, L. Meyers, and Elly the rehabber. Rebecca, thanks for the photographs and for your unwavering belief in the project. And to my family, thanks for riding along. Special thanks to Taylor, my long-suffering sheltie, who put up with my crow obsession when she would rather have been sniffing.

Notes for the Novice
Crow-watcher

Although the crow may be the first bird that most budding bird-watchers identify, I am often amazed at the number of people who confuse them with grackles, starlings, or ravens. All of these birds may be casually referred to as blackbirds, but only grackles and starlings belong to this diverse family called *Icteridae*. Ravens and crows are true cousins and members of the family *Corvidae*. Members of the family *Corvidae* or "Corvids" belong to an even larger group, the order Passeriformes, which designates perching birds. Members of the Corvid family—which includes crows, ravens, jays, magpies, jackdaws, and nutcrackers—are classified as songbirds. I know, quite a misnomer for singers with such questionable abilities.

The American crow, shiny and black, is decidedly larger than a grackle but smaller than a raven. Weighing in at one pound, the American crow measures approximately nineteen inches from beak to tail. Common grackles measure twelve-and-a-half inches long, by comparison, and ravens (the crow on steroids) a whopping twenty-five inches.

A group of crows is called a murder. Baby crows are called simps. But after watching these birds for any length of time, you will simply call them interesting.

Introduction: Wildlife Oasis in the City

I loved crows even before I knew I did. My feelings for them germinated like seeds waiting for the proper environment to emerge. I admired them from a distance, fascinated by their obvious intelligence. I never thought I'd have a chance to get close to them, as they are wary of people, and this characteristic only added to my attraction. They were mysterious and aloof. They drew me in, capturing my attention like a sudden flash of light in a dismal, gray world, much like most of the loves of my life.

I live in a large Midwestern city, a rather unlikely place for the study of nature, yet the beauty of urban wildlife inspires me. A soul that craves to befriend nature can find it anywhere, making the best of a less-than-perfect circumstance. Not very far from me are the great corporate industrial parks, with their "fake" lakes, manicured lawns, and dots of soldier-like trees intended to create an illusion, as if to help you forget the hostile concrete parking lots surrounding you. New strip malls crop up every other day, numbing humanity with their uniformity and draining the remaining charm from any small community that dares to try to hold on to its uniqueness.

Farther south, steel skyscrapers erupt from the earth. Tiny ruby-crowned kinglets and other migrating songbirds crash into their shiny reflective windows by the hundreds and fall to their deaths below. Pigeons, hunted by the introduced peregrine falcons, are hated for the sloppy mess they leave below their many roosts. I have heard it said that rats dance in the city streets after dark. I don't get down to the center of the city much, thus to me it is as foreign a place as it would be to a visitor from another state.

My yard has gradually turned from a postage stamp–sized lawn into a wildlife oasis, complete with a small pond and bird-friendly plantings. It offers respite from life in a maddening, noisy city. Here, the cars angrily boom a bass line as they circle the houses that huddle together in rows of anonymity. Far removed from the wilderness, I transform my home into a facsimile of a rustic cabin, bridging distance with wood and natural decorations. Conversely, I embrace the modernized advantages of gadgets and electronics—digital cameras, a piano that never needs tuning, and a computer that acts as a portal to the universe. I am grateful to be alive in an era in which so much information is available, in which my mind can reach wherever it might want. It is from this place and time that I write, to share with you my love of the American crow. (*Corvus brachyrhynchos*)

I do not fancy myself a writer or a scientist. I certainly pretend to be neither. I am a passionate observer, cataloging a subject I find compelling. I seek to honor the birds I love, clearing the misunderstanding of their negative stereotype. I want you to know crows as I know crows. This narrative contains my opinions, which are based on my observations. It is the story of a group of crows living near me, who over time have bestowed upon me the great honor of their friendship. It follows their daily lives, their relationships with each other, and the bond of trust I was able to forge with them, which allowed me a closer look at their secret world. Later, I introduce you to the captive crows I know and give you an insider's view of a wildlife rehabilitation center. If you are one of the few who share my passion and already appreciate crows, welcome. If you are willing to examine your preconceived notions, take a new look at these "common" birds.

PART I
Wild Crows

1

The Power of Peanuts

Parker Territory

MAINT.
GARAGE

TO W'S NEST AND ROOST

W Family Territory

RAILROAD TRACKS

PARK

FEEDING
ROOF

Scrap Family
Territory

SCHOOL
FIELD

A CROW'S EYE VIEW

It all started with a single peanut. I meant to attract blue jays to my garden so that I could photograph them. Instead, I received a greater gift—the one I really wanted but had not dared ask for. I had been hearing blue jays around the neighborhood, and, knowing they are fond of peanuts, I began tossing a few up on the garage roof as bait. By morning, the nuts would be gone. Who had found them? I hoped it was not a marauding group of squirrels. I liked the furry little creatures well enough, but I longed to have the noisy blue jewels instead. I decided to get up early one morning to see if I could catch a glimpse of who had found my lure.

Just before dawn, I entered the kitchen, and, to the sounds of my dog crunching at her kibble, I pried open the slats of the blinds on the back door. The sight of a jiggling blind might scare whatever was sneaking the nuts. I waited patiently, my muscles tensed from my willing them to be still.

What I saw that morning would forever change my life and delight me beyond my fondest hope. It wasn't blue jays or hungry squirrels. I watched as a big black bird landed on the peak of the garage roof and looked around nervously. Another swayed on the telephone wire above the yard, trying to gain his balance as he eyed the nuts by turning his head to one side. As the first bird grabbed one of the peanuts for himself, his friend on the wire was emboldened to land on the roof to claim his share.

What was so remarkable about seeing crows on the garage roof in the early morning hours? As a careful observer of nature, I was certain that I had never had a crow visit the garden before. Of course, there were crows in the park across the street and hanging around the field behind the school. I had heard their caws in the distance many times. But they were never more than fleeting specks at an insurmountable distance.

Where I lived, they proved elusive and wary. My attempts to approach them had been futile. Because they are a common bird, people harbor inaccurate recollections of shushing them aside with their shoe like broken glass or a discarded pop can. This may seem the case as you hurry to get somewhere, paying pay them little attention. However, should you really observe them or even photograph them, you would see how difficult it is to get close. They are much more aware of humans and attuned to our intent than vice versa.

Considering crows' long history of persecution by humans, it is no wonder that they do not trust us. Farmers blame them for eating their crops. Late-risers abhor them for their raucous morning calls. Sentimentalists cringe at their penchant for eating the young of other birds. Folklore casts them in an evil light, and Alfred Hitchcock evokes them as scary monsters. Some people just find them downright ugly.

In fact, I know of no other bird that so divides the camps of birders. You either love them or hate them. I rarely find birders who straddle the fence. I was, of course, a member of the former crowd. Crows had always been a source of wonder and mystery to me. Now here they were, right in my backyard.

It became my ritual to offer up five or so peanuts every evening as I sat out on the deck. I hoped this would coax my early-morning visitors to arrive at a more convenient time. I waited patiently, sometimes excluding my noisy dog, for a chance to see the crows in action. But they outsmarted me. I provided food every day, and it was eaten every day, but unless I got up at an ungodly hour, I didn't get to see the crows. It took a while for my feeble human mind to calculate what the crows already knew. It didn't matter what time I threw the nuts onto on the roof, since I could never retrieve them anyway. The crows knew they could come by at their convenience to get them. It was obvious they preferred to avoid me and had no interest in interacting with a complicated human. They followed their own agenda rather than mine. It seemed they had the upper hand.

While out walking, I was vigilant, scanning the trees for crows and paying close attention to my surroundings. I learned early on that if a crow does not want to be detected, it won't be. A black shape blends easily with the shadows of summer foliage or successfully camouflages itself against a tree limb in winter.

I did, however, begin to detect a pattern of crow sightings near the corner of the park. I saw them on the telephone lines above the railroad tracks or casting about on the ground in search of something. I could not be sure that these were the crows that were taking the nuts, as, in the early days, I had no real idea how crows lived or spent their time.

About a month after I began the peanut routine, I was scanning a large sycamore on my neighbor's lawn with my binoculars. I wasn't looking for crows, just any interesting bird to break up the world of sparrows at my feet. So it was a shock to spot her there, looking back at me. She studied me, as I did her, first turning her head one way and then the other. She wiped the branch at her feet brusquely with her beak and continued to appraise my action. I couldn't be sure, but I thought it must be one of the crows responsible for the missing peanuts. It was the first time I had ever seen a crow perched in this particular tree, which offered a perfect vantage point for watching the garage roof.

As I continued to study the crow, it became difficult to hold the binoculars steady, but I couldn't put them down. How would I be able to tell if this was the same crow, should I ever see her again? I strained to find anything to help me remember her. It was when she turned her head again that I noticed a small triangular patch of white next to her eye. She must have lost some feathers in this spot, giving me a detail I could use to identify her in the future.

Even an avid crow lover can get bored staring at a near-motionless crow in a tree, and so I went inside for the evening. It wasn't long after that the nuts disappeared.

My long vigils began to pay off in mid-August 1999. I would set out my bait and wait, and soon a crow would begin a series of what I called "fly-bys." Coming from the direction of the park, he would make a wide circle, check the roof for nuts, look to see me alert at my post, and then move on past me. I celebrated this tiny bit of progress. The crows had put me on their regular route; they weren't just hiding in the trees anymore.

One evening when the small-fry baseball teams had finally cleared the park and quiet reigned once again, I took my bossy little sheltie for a walk. On our way home, I heard sudden caws erupt from the wires over the railroad tracks. Three crows were sitting near each other on the wires, and they seemed to be cawing at me! One in particular was very agitated. He flicked his wing and tail feathers rapidly, and wiped his beak on the line. His friend mimicked this beak-wiping gesture. I was not quite convinced that this show was for my benefit, and I looked around for another cause. Suddenly, all three crows flew toward me, landing on the streetlight just as I was passing it. Their action seemed more than a coincidence. I was still trying to digest what was happening, when, just as suddenly, they flew ahead of me to the maple tree directly in front of my house. I counted five crows in the tree, and they were all eyes as I passed them.

The crows seemed to have told me by their actions that they recognized me and that they knew where I lived. It is not unusual for crows, or even other wild birds, to recognize people as individuals. Kevin McGowan, a biologist who studies crows in Ithaca, notes that his research activities have caused all the crows in the area not only to recognize him but also to "hate" him. He is unpopular with the crows for his disturbance of their young as he climbs trees to tag the helpless looking Corvids in the nest.

This act by my local crows signaled a willingness on their part to acknowledge me. Perhaps they were curious about me. On the other hand, perhaps it was a crow gesture of friendship, the beginning of a trust built on my willingness to provide treats without demanding anything in return. I based my actions and expectations of the local crows on this protocol. I knew it would take much patience and time to interact with a wild creature.

Soon after this incident, I was out for another walk in the park. Before leaving home, I had tossed a handful of nuts onto the garage roof. The crows, which I had begun to recognize as *my* crows, were foraging near a large mud puddle that formed every time it rained in what would be right field of the Little League baseball diamond. As soon as the three crows spotted me, they flew directly to the garage roof to collect their nuts. Their tiny brains had foiled me again! They had figured out that if they saw me walking in the park, I would not be sitting in my deck chair scrutinizing them, and they had seized the opportunity to retrieve the nuts.

This incident confirmed my suspicion that the crows could in fact recognize me by sight. I wondered how they did it. Did we humans all look alike to them? Was it my dog they were discriminating? Perhaps they just watched the house I came from, and identified me in this way.

I thought it quite clever of them to take advantage of my absence from the deck to filch the nuts. It appeared that they had formulated a clever plan. Because they repeated this behavior many times in the period before we became friends, I would conclude that it was more than a mere coincidence.

I understood that any wild creature—and especially crows—might be suspicious of my motives, but it occurred to me that they might not understand that I was leaving nuts for them on purpose. Maybe they thought they were stealing from me or believed that my leaving the food out was in no way connected to them—just as I was unsure their activities were in any way related to me. This revelation would be a turning point in my relationship with them. For whether my instincts were right or wrong, the next actions I took had a positive effect.

I began a campaign to make the crows understand that I intended the nuts specifically for them and that I meant them no harm. I began carrying a pocketful of nuts at all times. Whenever I heard or saw crows, whether out my back window or at the park, I dropped what I was doing, and brought nuts to them. I saw the crows most often on my walks through the park. I kept my distance but made sure they saw my offering. I would place the nut on a clear patch of ground, where it would be easy to see, and then look up to make sure they were watching me. I was patient, and I never demanded anything in return. I respected whatever distance the crows felt comfortable with and never stood watching for them to take the treat, as they might construe my surveillance as a trap. With my actions I said, "Take this as a gift." I never let up.

Body language was important—both theirs and mine. I watched them closely for any signs that I was getting too close. My goal was to avoid scaring them into flying off. I did not stare at them. I kept a relaxed posture. In addition, I learned by the errors I made. For example, swinging my arm to toss them a nut, even from a safe distance, caused them to flee in fear. Their agitated screams pierced my heart and made me feel I had lost the ground I'd gained. Nevertheless, they forgave me in time as I learned more about them.

Eventually, they were quicker to come out when they saw me and quicker to come get the nuts after I left them. I began to shape their behavior. I stopped giving nuts to any crows that were hiding from me, even if I could spot them in the trees. I pretended I didn't know they were there, and this taught them to come out in plain view when they saw me. The streetlights that lined the park were ideal perches. It wasn't long before they not only flew directly to these the posts when they saw me but used them as begging spots to let me know they were around and available to be fed.

I could see several of the streetlights from inside the house, and I always came out when I saw the crows perched on them. In this way, we influenced each other's behavior. They became my spoiled pets as I began including scraps from my kitchen with the nuts. I saved bits of meat, fat, bones, and pizza for them. They seemed happy with all of it—after getting over their initial fear and distrust of the new foods.

Birds in general are wary of novel food items. Their parents teach them what to eat, and it is a protective measure to be so careful. Wariness, after all, could prevent them from eating poison. Anyone who has tried to offer a pet bird a new food has experienced this fear firsthand. In the crows, their caution manifested as reluctance to approach the food and a maneuver ornithologists coined "jump backs." The crow appeared to sneak toward the item in a low crouch, and as it got close, it sprang back as if touching a live wire. As its fear of the item receded, it got braver in its poking and less electric when jumping back. Eventually, it reconciled the novelty and ventured to taste it. Usually, it was a tiny little bite followed by a thoughtful look as it swallowed, as though it were saying, "Hmmm, will I like this?" If the answer was yes, (and it usually was), the crow would carry the piece away or begin ripping at it immediately.

As crows are extremely adaptable and well-known for foraging in garbage dumps, they might be less resistant than other birds to trying new food items. These crows had probably come across similar items already, having lived in close contact with humanity. Crows are omnivores. Their natural diet consists of worms, bugs, small mammals, eggs, nestlings, nuts, grains, and human garbage.

It didn't take long for my original targets—the blue jays—to figure out that there were peanuts on the menu. Because they were much bolder than the crows, they often took advantage of their competitors' reluctance to take the nuts when I was present. The jays snatched up nuts at an alarming rate. I couldn't tell how many blue jays I had visiting; it could have been two or it could have been seven.

I was glad to feed them, but, secretly, I began rooting for the crows to win out. The jays never paused to inspect the nuts, as I had seen the crows do; they had an impatient attitude, as though the very speed at which they moved could keep them from any harm. It seemed a good strategy, and they became regular blue flashes through the garden.

The sparrows in my yard reacted to the presence of these predator Corvids. Especially keen to protect their nests, they sounded a distinctive alarm call when any Corvids were present. I listened for their chattering and used it as an early warning system that the crows were in the vicinity. Sparrows were much more skilled at spotting the crows than I would ever be, and their vantage points up in the trees allowed them to see what I couldn't. Soon I learned to recognize that the sparrows had unique alarms depending on which predator was threatening. The American kestrel caused them to use a shrill whistle like chirp, the location of which was hard to detect. For although the brave bird that spots the predator protects his flock mates by calling out, he puts himself in significant danger by broadcasting his location. The sparrow has the ability to throw his voice like a ventriloquist.

Blue jays, on the other hand, usually elicited a chattering type of scolding. All the sparrows in the area would join in this chant and line up in force on telephone lines and in small groups to advertise the strength of their numbers. Sometimes the jay would be mobbed and chased, and other times this show was enough to deter the jay from stealing babies or eggs from a nest. Sometimes it was not. It acted only as a fire alarm sounding futilely as the building burned to the ground. It is a sad sight to see a blue jay flying off with a young naked nestling in his beak, but it is also a necessity of nature I had come to accept.

Most useful was the alarm the sparrows used to exclaim, "Watch it, the crows are here." Like hiring hundreds of little research assistants, they worked without pay, all day long. I could concentrate on other things while outside and always be assured that my little workers would let me know if the crows were in the vicinity.

I tuned my spirit to the sparrows in this way, listening for each nuance in their calls. It made me feel a part of the flock. I could hear when fights broke out, and I cringed at the sound of an offending birds' toe being tweaked. I heard the heartbreak in their frantic protests as young were lost to predation, and I felt my stomach twist at their fear of the shadowy hawk in the sky.

2

The First Family

I determined that I had four separate crows to account for in the group I had begun to think of as my own. There was another group of crows, living in what appeared to be a separate gathering and defending a boundary line adjacent to them. I could easily tell which crows belonged to which grouping by the direction they flew. My group inhabited the corner of the park and flew west from the garden. The other crows, possible interlopers to the territory, flew south toward the field. They seemed to call that area home.

The visual markers I used to distinguish individual crows were becoming more familiar to me as I practiced looking for them. "Triangle Eye," the crow with the missing patch of feathers, practiced her nightly ritual of sitting in the tree in my line of sight. She seemed more watchful than the others. "Polka-Dot Spy" was a friendly sort who showed the most interest in me and who was distinguished by a polka-dot molt pattern on his belly feathers. Sometimes when crows molt, they are left with white patches of downy feathers on their bellies and breasts, which gives them a mottled appearance. They can look quite ragged—like sloppy dressers—until their sleek black feathers return. One crow limped noticeably, and the fourth crow had a rather rounded beak, which gave his face a sweet expression. The crows needed proper names.

I began making quick sketches of any notable feather abnormalities and molting marks. This method proved useless, however, because the crows moved quickly and their feathers could change by the day. Through my failure, I learned to rely on behavior rather than appearance, and it remained the best indicator of individuals. I used the transient physical markers more as confirmation of my initial thoughts on the identity of the crow in question.

To imply that this was a simple, foolproof method is beyond a stretch. In addition, to imply that I was always sure which crow was which would be a lie. Nevertheless, I did improve at identifying the individuals, especially under optimum conditions. After a great deal of observation, I was eventually able to understand the differences between the crows on some level I find difficult to explain—perhaps in the same way a mother knows instantly which identical twin is which, whereas strangers might struggle. There were times I was able to look at a crow perched in a tree and have a gut feeling who it was, only to amaze myself when more reliable measures validated my guess. Perhaps I unconsciously noticed some behavior or another clue that tipped my intuition.

Since crows are sexually monochromatic, the only sure way to tell male from female is with a blood or feather DNA test. Scientists using measurements of feathers and beaks have found that males on average are slightly larger than their female counterparts. Firsthand observation of crows mating would be another informal gender clue. For the purpose of this narrative, and to reconcile the puzzle in my own mind, I made some educated guesses on the sex of my crow group. I hoped fervently for a day when I might know these things as fact, but until then, I was left with my best conjecture.

I supplemented my theoretical wanderings with all the reading material I could find on the American crow. I studied up on ravens and blue jays, their close cousins, for any insights I might glean. Based on this material, I began to form ideas about the crows I had before me.

The uninitiated crow-watcher might believe that the crows flying through their neighborhood at any given time are a steady parade of new birds. However, crows live in stable family groups that usually consist of a breeding pair and offspring from previous nests. This family unit defends a home territory, keeping out interloping crows. The offspring can stay for up to six years and act as helpers to their parents, who, it is believed, mate for life.

In some areas of the country, late fall and winter brings a change in the family structure, as more crows join together in large foraging flocks. With no duties to a nest or fledglings to care for, the crows seek the company of a larger aggregate. Crows old enough to breed may also use this time to search for a mate for the coming season. However, studies using devices to track and monitor crows' activities find that crows with an established territory still spend a part of the day there.

The four crows I was watching seemed to be a family unit. It was on this assumption that I began building my ideas of their relationships to each other. A name for the first crow I sought to identify came easily. In memory of the gentle pig in the book *Charlotte's Web*, I chose Wilbur as the name for the crow I thought might be the male of the breeding pair. His sweet nature was reminiscent of his namesake. Clearly the boldest of the bunch, he was the first to swoop down for food on the roof. The first to trust me, he allowed the gap between us to narrow and skittered away less quickly if I was near. He was the second largest crow, although feather fluffing can make it nearly impossible to judge such things. He also had a certain rasp to his cawing that set him apart from the others.

The fact that these crows seemed to follow a pecking order when feeding on my roof made things easier to sort. The second crow down was always the one I had called Polka-Dot Spy. I decided to call him Willy. The name evoked a picture of easygoing friendliness. I suspected he was a helper from a previous nest. I knew he was at least a year old, since the inside of his mouth was black and not the characteristic red of a younger bird. Therefore, he could not have been a fledgling from this year's nest. I assumed him male based on some indications that rank breaks on gender lines, with males more dominant. Willy, I felt, was the male offspring of the mated pair or possibly even Wilbur's brother. However, I did not see in his actions the hint that he was the partner to any of the others in the group. Scientists studying tagged crows have found that brothers often live together, keeping an allegiance and family bond even after one of them pairs off.

The third crow that came down to the roof was the one I had been calling Triangle Eye—if she bothered to come down at all, that is. Many times, she would wait until Wilbur and Willy had gathered the goods, and then she would fly off to where they were and mooch some of their stash. They did not mind one bit and readily shared with her. It seemed to be her role to watch carefully for my arrival and subsequent food offers. She became vigilant about waiting for me in the morning, always waking before I did and taking up her post on the telephone lines above the garage. When the food was there, she called to the boys, alerting them with short staccato notes in her excited voice. She preferred keeping her post to coming near to me, and her standoffish nature did not change, even as the others warmed to me. I called her Winona and believed she was Wilbur's mate.

The final crow was the easiest to name, as his disability provided a fitting moniker. It was hard to know what was wrong with Limpy's leg, but he always favored it. My untrained eye told me it was out of pain and not paralysis. This characteristic would be quite a hindrance to a creature that must spend most of its forage time walking along looking for bugs in the grass. Perhaps Limpy's leg was one reason he was my best customer at feeding times. But he wore it well. He was the lovable hog, always willing to take advantage of free food. I was glad I could fill his stomach, after what could quite have possibly been a long dry spell.

Without knowing why, I began to think of Limpy as a respected elder within the family. Perhaps his wizened, tattered appearance added to this impression. Interesting to note was the fact that he was allowed to pass easily between the two separate groups of crows. While he foraged in the south field, indicating that he was welcome in the group of crows who lived there, I saw him many times also perching next to my family of crows. He seemed to be gladly received in either circle. Was Limpy being helped or tolerated because of his leg? (Many wild creatures shun the injured, so as not to weaken the group as a whole.) Was there a common familial lineage between the groups with Limpy being the link? Could he have been connected by virtue of a crow marriage?

One Sunday morning, Limpy was hanging out with my home group, whom I referred to as the "W" family, having named all but Limpy using this letter of the alphabet. Things between us had been progressing well, and the crows seemed comfortable keeping me in their line of sight while relaxing in the trees. That morning, they had just finished the breakfast I had fixed them and were sitting in an evergreen directly over my neighbor's garage. I sat drinking coffee as I watched them doze lazily or preen first one wing feather then the next. I was so close to them, I could almost hear the snap of their primaries as they drew them quickly through their beaks and they sprang back into place. It was becoming a ritual for them to sit near me even when they were not asking me for food. It was a great compliment for me to be allowed to enjoy their company in this way.

I wondered if our trust level had advanced to the point where I might drag out my camera with its ominous-looking telephoto lens. Struggling against the inertia of a perfectly beautiful day, I quietly slid into the house to fetch it, hoping my movement would not cause the crows to take leave and spoil my plan. To my surprise, not only did they stay put, they allowed me to point the rather large and scary-looking implement in their direction. They looked on with interest at what I was doing. I focused, fiddled, and snapped, hoping to keep track in my mind of which crow I was photographing. They posed patiently, turning their heads from side to side like vain stars at a publicity shoot. They even seemed to take turns sitting on the center branch, as though they somehow knew this was the focal point of my aim. I was surprised that they were not frightened of an object that so resembles the barrel of a gun. Perhaps I had passed their very stringent tests and had gained some level of their confidence. If in fact they were beginning to view me as purveyor of good things, maybe they thought the strange machine I had might benefit them in some way. I have often wondered if they pondered our customs, as I pondered theirs. Could they contemplate travel in our automobiles, for example, as we wondered how it must feel to fly?

Today, viewing these photos of Limpy and the W's is bittersweet, as that day was one of the last times I ever saw my friend Limpy. I can only guess that his disappearance was attributable to his handicap. Life in the wild is difficult even for the perfect specimen. I was glad for the chance to know Limpy.

Soon after Limpy's departure, the W's and I had a major breakthrough. I was used to dropping their treats and leaving them or even tossing them from a distance as the W's sat on the light posts lining the park. But one day, I bounced a grape toward Wilbur, and he immediately dropped down, folding his wings and hurtling toward the ground like a stone. He took several steps toward me and pierced the grape with his beak, quietly eating it as I stood watching from only a few feet away. When he was finished, I tossed another grape toward him, and, like a veteran shortstop, he ran forward and snatched it up with his beak. It was the first time he had trusted me enough to take the food as I tossed it to him, without hesitation. Willy soon followed suit, while Winona looked on from above. The events stunned me, coming with no prior indication that the W's had been ready to move to this next level. Even Winona eventually joined in. This episode marked the beginning of a new era in which the crows began to actively seek the friendship I offered.

Vacations, weekends, and flexible work schedules allowed me the time to sit on my deck at unpredictable times. Willy adapted by doing regular reconnaissance missions over the yard, checking for me while cruising by, never knowing when I might have the rest of a tuna sandwich to share. Once, obviously surprised to see me, he slammed on his brakes by pulling his feet toward his chest and resisting the air with them so he could do a double take. He looked like a cartoon bird.

Sometimes Willy landed directly above me on a wire ten feet or so above as I sat on the deck. I was amazed at how quietly he approached; I often felt a presence and looked up to find him perched there. I began speaking to him in a small whisper, hoping to reach him without arousing the quizzical stares of any neighbors within earshot. Mostly I said hello, and asked how he was, and wondered aloud if he could understand my intent. He indulged me, and even seemed to listen as a pet might, meeting my gaze in a way that let me know he was present. He wasn't always asking for food, as evidenced by the fact that he didn't immediately take what I tossed for him, although no food ever went to waste on the roof.

Willy loved scrambled eggs even more than the others did. He had a way of tucking his head and running toward me that served as an early indicator of his identity. Wilbur and Winona usually strolled or, if in a hurry to catch up, half hopped and half flew low to the ground. I began to keep a list of individual quirks that could help me tell the crows apart.

Another pattern I noticed was perch choice. Just as we might tend toward a favorite chair at home or a usual seat in a restaurant, the crows preferred certain perches to others. Winona liked the neighbor's sycamore tree, while Wilbur often perched on the telephone line strung over the yard. All three liked the highest branches of the maple in my front yard and the wires over the railroad tracks.

As I made note of the crows' patterns, they in turn took note of mine. They knew when I walked the dog; they knew when I left for work. They knew that when my garage door opened, I had arrived home. They knew that if my dog barked in the yard, I couldn't be far behind. And they knew that when the lights in the house went on in the morning, I was awake and would be available for feeding duty.

In fact, Wilbur took to perching on my neighbor's roof and looking into my kitchen window as I fixed breakfast for my dog and pet bird. I never felt he was hurrying me, but I took comfort in his appearance each morning, knowing that no matter the turn of events in my personal life, a faithful crow would always brighten at the sight of me. I brightened myself at the sight of Wilbur's clear eyes and gently rounded beak. It was as though nature had manifested this crow's personality by endowing him with such an appendage, rather than the sharp and pointy weapon that most people associate with a crow's temperament.

My experience with the crows was showing me the true nature of a bird often scorned. The crows were doglike, both in faithfulness and loyalty. They developed feelings for me that were as easy to sense as the love of a pet. They anticipated and enjoyed our interactions, displaying a level of connectedness akin to true friendship.

3

The Language of Crows

What is all the cawing about? Do crows talk to each other in a complex and detailed way, or are their calls limited to a few broad categories: finding mates; defending territory; and warning, mobbing or contacting others? The ability to mimic vocal patterns marks the beginnings of a language. The crows I was tracking called back and forth, repeating each other's vocal patterns, on a regular basis. Most of these instances were between the W's and their neighbors in the south field. How could I determine what these sounds meant? What nonverbal signals did they also employ?

Crows are capable of some twenty-three different sounds, ranging from the obvious caws to rattles and more mammalian moans and coos. Several of their vocalizations are quiet and reserved for intimates.

Like listening to a foreign language, in time, their sounds became more familiar to me, and I was able to recognize variations in the calls of the W family. My interpretations depended upon season, context, and the individual bird. I gained insight by learning to differentiate the tenor of the call—from staccato urgency to casual drawn-out rasps. It was easy for me to recognize the alarmed calls of a bird discovering a predatory hawk near by. Confirmation of this interpretation came when all the local crows gathered to help drive off the threat. Other sounds were much more difficult to unravel. I believe that even the most learned of crow scholars would admit that true knowledge of the language of crows is beyond us—that is until we discover a way to get inside the birds' heads. As I puzzled over the sounds I heard, I thought of the times the crows had directed their communications to me, their human friend. In addition to the auditory communications, I noted several crow behaviors that I interpreted based on my interactions with them.

Willy and Winona began talking to me when they learned that it could bring me out of the house or attract my attention if I had missed seeing them. "Caw, caw, caw," I would hear, as they leaned low on the wires to spy on me in the kitchen. Sometimes they would sound off from the streetlight in front of the house, as though wondering if I was home, although many times they already knew I was. I reinforced this behavior by acknowledging them with a treat. In a similar vein, the variation of the contact call, "Ka kuk, ka kuk," with the second syllable rising in tone, came to remind me of the human phrase, "Come here." The crows used this call without urgency; it was a request more than a demand. "Look at this," it seemed to say. As any birdcalls are extremely difficult to describe with words alone, I have included many of the vocalizations mentioned in this book on the Web site CawOfTheWild.com.

I found that wing and tail flicking, the rapid jerking motion of the wings away from the body, and fanning of the tail, could help crows locate each other in a tangle of branches. The gestures reminded me of waving, "I'm over here." Eminent bird researcher Lawrence Kilham notes this kind of movement as a sign of a nervous bird who is ready to take action. I would concur but also reiterate that context is always important. A crow flicking its wings and wiping its beak rapidly on its perch, while watching a companion picking through the grass below, might be expressing its irritation that its stash of food is being stolen. Yet, when the crows called out to me after I had inadvertently passed their perch without seeing them and then flicked their wings when I turned around, it allowed me to locate them in an otherwise camouflaged spot.

Beak wiping and picking at branches or leaves in an irritated fashion is thought to be a displacement activity, even in pet birds. When experiencing a strong emotion—such as anger—the bird seems to manifest its feelings through movement. Rather than attacking another bird for a perceived transgression, the bird takes its anger out on an inanimate object.

I also noticed that crows living in family groups sometimes used their head and beaks to strike odd poses that appeared to mean something to them. They turned their heads and pointed their beaks at strange angles, holding these postures for several moments and, at times, acting as if they were in some sort of trance. Occasionally they would use their beaks to poke lightly at each other. It seemed to me in these moments that they were sharing an intense emotional exchange. Sometimes they opened their beaks slightly, and sometimes they flashed their inner eyelids or nictitating membranes. I called this activity "strange statues."

Strange Statues

Nonverbal signals seemed to play an especially important role at close range. I have seen both the wild and captive crows I know use this eyelid flash to communicate interest and involvement in whatever they are focusing on at the moment. This bluish white covering showed in sharp contrast to the crows' black feathers. The flashing of the nictitating membrane signaled to me a heightened emotional state. In my experience, it is generally a positive signal, communicating affection or enjoyment. I watch carefully for this subtle sign.

Fluffing the feathers of the head is another way a crow can show its state of mind. Excitement and related emotions seem to be indicated in this way. In some instances—like grinning ear-to-ear in humans—this gesture shows joy, or even affection.

Another method crows have used to communicate with me nonverbally is to fly low over my head to let me know of their presence—and as a gesture of friendliness. I have never felt the least bit threatened by this action, as it has never been an aggressive swoop but a low, slow glide. Actually, to be greeted in this way thrilled me and made me feel included in their circle. In other cases, one crow swooped over another to gain its attention or to encourage the bird to follow.

A more aggressive use of this same action intimidates rivals, as I saw while watching competition between the family groups in my area. Such "dive-bombing" can serve equally well to drive other crows—or even predators—away. As a member of one group dive-bombed a member of the other, the victim would flatten itself on the ground, wings away from its body, sometimes with its beak open in a fledgling begging posture. I interpreted this action as equivalent to a canine rolling onto its back, the message being, "Don't hurt me."

Begging

This low crouch wing fluttering posture is used by young birds and mates begging food or by subordinates attacked by aggressors

Another maneuver used in aggressive interaction between crows involved one crow trying to fly its pursuer into a stationary object. If, for example, Winona gave chase in a territory dispute with a neighbor, the other bird would speed toward the fence surrounding the baseball diamond, as though he might be heading for a collision. At the last moment, he would pull up, hoping Winona would be distracted enough by the pursuit to crash. I have seen this action enough times to believe it is not a coincidental occurrence but a deliberate strategy to discourage or injure the pursuing bird.

Crow Crash Trick

Interactions between the neighboring groups of crows were frequent. They cawed to keep the boundaries of their respective territories cohesive or called to one another across boundaries, seemingly to exchanging information important to a crow. In some cases, these calls kept outsider groups at bay and, in others, drew the larger whole together. Although crows have allegiance to a family group first, they still form collectives for the sake of the greater good. Mobbing their common enemies serves to unite them regardless of territory or family affiliations.

For all their bravado against larger enemies and despite their reputations as bullies, crows appear to be neurotic and fearful birds. Whether uttering an urgent and rhythmic alarm call—"Kek, kek, kek"—or a full-blown hysterical scream, a crow voices its frequent fear of the environment. This warning, or fear call, could indicate anything from a prowling cat to a Styrofoam cup blowing in the wind.

In fact, one day Wilbur and his family became panic-stricken when a cup of this type, thrown from a car window, rolled haplessly in half circles beneath the streetlight. Hearing the commotion, I hurried over to see what they were upset about, as they hunched together above me. Expecting an evil monster, I was surprised to find the harmless cup. I quickly scooped it up and, tossing it into the trash, hoped I had shown my usefulness and loyalty to the crows by dispensing with this offending item. I think even Winona was impressed with my great power.

Wilbur displayed the greatest variety of calls in his family, at least within my earshot. There were several days running when I heard geese honking in the distance as Wilbur approached for breakfast. Eventually I discovered that it was Wilbur, sounding off as he came in for a landing on his favorite wire over the yard. He was getting quite used to me, and I stared up at him in wonder as he eyed the leftover chicken in my hands. He seemed willing to communicate with me and bring me into his world, explaining his ways in the only fashion he knew how. I do not know if the honking sound he used is a natural crow sound or if he was mimicking the real geese he had met. It was fall after all, and the geese were in flight. Why did he choose this particular call to greet me in the mornings? Was he telling me where he had been all night? "I was in the place of geese," said Wilbur, and I thought of the cemetery and the golf course near by. Could Wilbur have just been playing at being a goose, imitating their call as he flew in? Perhaps, having a full-service restaurant had freed up his creative, playful side.

I do not know what made Wilbur try to bridge the gap between human and crow. Perhaps he is just the expressive sort, like the type of person who likes to let you know what he's thinking. One morning, as Wilbur was sitting on the wire over the yard, waiting for me to throw his breakfast, he bent his neck, as if bowing to me, and quietly clacked his beak several times. I had no idea what this meant, but my gut told me it was some sort of greeting. It certainly seemed a friendly gesture and not aggressive in any way. I was happy with this interpretation for a long time, until one day, I saw a lone crow clacking this way before he settled in to eat. Since that time, having observed this behavior many times in the context of eating, I have come to believe it is not a greeting at all. Rather, it appears to refer to food. After Wilbur first introduced this gesture, I noticed it in all the crows I watched, whether they were known to me or strangers, wild or captive. Sometimes they signaled to other crows, and sometimes the gesture was used when they were alone, almost as when a human exclaims, "Ooh, I'm hungry," or "Let's eat."

Wilbur's action that day was even more interesting because he combined two gestures, bowing and clacking. I have come to believe the bow *is* a greeting. Wilbur continued to bow to me occasionally, and I sometimes bent my neck in return. A few times, he even responded when I initiated a bow, but it is hard to know if it were something he would have done anyway. I do not know in what context this greeting is used or if it is more than a simple hello. The crow might be overcome by some emotion that causes him to react this way. The gesture does remind me of the posture used to solicit preening from another bird.

Wilbur's Greeting

Bow   Clack

It was endearing to have Wilbur talk to me as though he were communicating his feelings. It was while chatting with Wilbur that I learned of his distaste for rollerblades. Each time a rollerblader passed under his perch, he barked disapprovingly. It sounded like an irritated grumble, almost a cough. I have since heard it used to express reproach among other crows.

Wilbur shared with me some other unique sounds as well. "Ch, sh, sh," he said one day. I was the only other creature within earshot, so I assumed this call was for my benefit. I had no idea what it meant until I caught myself making a similar sound to stop my dog from barking at the crows. Was Wilbur copying me? Was he trying to say something to me about my dog? He made this "comment" on a day when my sheltie had not accompanied me. Was he just making a sound from my language that he thought I might understand? Or was he asking me where my noisy companion was?

It was upon a framework of scientific literature and personal observation that I began to build my understanding of the complicated lives of crows.

4

Four-and-Twenty Black Birds Eating Pizza Pie

Caching food surplus is a common practice among the Corvid family. Other birds, such as the black-capped chickadee, also engage in this behavior. The W's spent considerable energy caching, uncaching, and recaching bits of food. Sometimes this activity seemed without purpose. Sometimes, however, it was clearly in response to the persistent, exasperating squirrels, who followed the crows around, stealing the nuts they had cached. The crows mostly ignored the squirrels or became only mildly annoyed. They seemed to accept the routine as a part of life. Sometimes they tried to fake the squirrels out, but a sleight of beak is no match for a squirrel's nose.

They also tolerated the squirrels that occasionally showed up on the roof as I was handing out nuts. The crows and I tried to communicate strategies to fool them. As we made eye contact, trying to out-think the squirrels and to bridge the gap somehow between our own minds, we realized the futility. After all, the squirrels were usually faster on the draw, less afraid, and hungrier than my well-fed crows.

I only saw Wilbur get truly cross with a squirrel once. All he had to do was assume a threatening posture and make a small gruff sound, and the squirrel became immediately submissive. Considering the history of food pilfering and the fact that squirrels are known nest predators of crows, the relationship was remarkably tolerant.

The three crows in the W family seemed to have favorite spots for their personal cache, almost as though they each had a shelf in the refrigerator. Willy most often chose the railroad tracks, while Wilbur and Winona staked out separate patches of the right field area in the baseball diamond. Sometimes all three would carry large pieces, like rib bones, to the factory roofs adjacent to the tracks. Since I had never seen a squirrel up there, it may have been a way of keeping special bits away from the furry moochers. I often wondered if the crows placed less precious morsels in the places where they would most likely be pilfered first. Perhaps they were feeding their pet squirrels, while still saving the best morsels for themselves. It certainly seemed as though thought went into the placement of these caches, as the crows paused often as though to consider things.

I could see their discrimination most clearly when a crow landed on the garage roof and carefully made his selection from the assortment. After weighing the options, he would often hesitate while looking first in one direction and then the other. I could almost read his intent while watching his head and eye movements. Weighing the options was often more literal than figurative. Like choosy mothers in the grocery store, the crows would pick up and drop one nut after the other before selecting the best of the bunch. Many bird species use weight as an indicator of quality or stage of ripeness. In peanuts, it is easy to tell if the meats have rotted or shriveled by the lightness of the whole. Why bother with the useless ones?

Wilbur acted as though he were in a buffet line. It was often easy to spot him, as he made a habit of taking one of each type of food offered for the day. Stacking them one atop the other, he made a Dagwoodesque pile. One fry, one fish piece, and one peanut, and off he would fly, presumably to sort them. Willy and Winona were more likely to stick to their favorite items, taking all of one item even if offered a variety.

Each day, the crows performed a balancing act, seeing how much they could stuff into their beaks and carry off without dropping the pile. Time-management and efficiency seemed lost on them, since a number of times stacks of food would spew out of their overloaded beaks, and they would have to start the process from scratch. It would seem a bird this intelligent would quickly admit that three was the highest number of nuts a crow could manage in one haul. This bit of reasoning seemed to escape them, however, or perhaps they felt it more important to take the risk and gather as much as they could while standing on the roof, lest a competitor take the best pieces while they were gone.

Another technique they sometimes employed was the use of what I call "temporary holding stations." Hiding the food in a nearby spot was a way of claiming certain pieces as their own. They often created a stash in the metal vent cap on top of the garage roof. In the winter, they carelessly shoved food into the snow on the next roof over. These bits were later properly cached as time allowed, usually after the initial process of removing all of the food from the garage roof.

The crows spent a fair amount of time scavenging in the grass at the park and walking along the railroad tracks across the way. I watched carefully through field glasses as Willy tucked a peanut under a tuft of grass, and then searched for just the right scrap of leaf to mark the treasure. He arranged the leaf several times before he was satisfied with the result. To my eye, it was a dance of aimlessness—this walking about in the grass, poking and prodding—but to the crows these searches yielded a tasty bug or a bit of chicken stowed the day before.

One thing I never worried about was rotting food left to attract vermin on the roof. Once the crows learned the schedule, they were quick to remove it. That is unless, of course, they found my cooking objectionable that day. This was a rare occurrence for a crow, and I took it personally when it did happen. To think they would rather pick through the garbage dump or eat beetles left little doubt as to my culinary skills. Once I prepared what I thought would be a veritable crow delicacy. I had some left over corn. I had some leftover pancake batter. Voilà! Crow Pancakes! But my spoiled crows snubbed them. Weren't crows supposed to love corn? Were Heckle and Jeckle just another myth of my youth? The crows looked at the pancakes and then at me. "You burned these," their disdain said. OK, they were a little blackened but were they really worthy of this insult? A pancake even a crow would refuse?

Cooking for crows was a responsibility I took seriously, as by feeding them I was saving them from eating natural, healthier foods. Nature was the Whole Foods Market; I was the corner hot dog stand. I tried in vain to eat healthy foods, but, like the crows, I craved pepperoni. I tried to justify my behavior with the knowledge that if the crows didn't get their junk food from me, they would surely find it themselves in a fast food parking lot. Who had never seen a crow picking up french fries near a dumpster?

Willy had honed to a fine art the practice of raiding McDonald's bags. I discovered this talent once when I saw him throwing one of the recognizable bags into the air repeatedly, thereby shaking loose the fries imprisoned inside. Winona recognized powdered-sugar donuts so quickly that I thought she must have a favorite donut shop on her route.

That said, I never gave them old or spoiled food or anything that I wouldn't eat. And I certainly never considered feeding them stale bread that fills them up but provides little nutrition. Their favorite foods are meat, meat, and meat. They love meat of any kind. Pizza means it's a red-letter day. In the winter, sometimes I would scramble eggs for them. It's difficult, after all, to throw spaghetti onto a roof. I am, in fact, the only person I know with food stains on the side of my garage. I am quite certain, however, that I was never providing the totality of the crows' diet, as I saw them shopping for worms and other delicacies on a regular basis.

Crows have a pouch behind their tongues in which they can store food that they can later spit out. They use the pouch as a sort of carryall, and as it becomes full, you begin to see a bulge in the crow's throat. This *antelingual* pouch—from the Latin meaning "behind the tongue"—is an intriguing bit of crow biology. Imagine comfortably swallowing a whole peanut—shell intact—without gagging, holding it in your throat, and then expelling it later when you found a place to cache it. This area is also sometimes referred to as a "gular pouch," and resembles the hanging pouch of a pelican on a smaller scale.

The W family never fought or scrapped over food within their family circle. They were very tolerant of each other and most times polite about the whole process. The sparrows and cardinals that shared a sunflower feeder in the garden below were much more aggressive toward each other in competition for food. The cardinals in my yard did not live up to their retiring reputation and never allowed the sparrows to intimidate them into leaving. They commandeered the feeder perch, opening their beaks in threat, hissing like cats, and lunging at any other bird that dared try to feed next to them. The sparrows scrapped back, both within their own species and with the cardinals. These little birds were feisty. Crows, on the other hand, might race each other to get to a favored piece, but once one had reached it, they played fair, allowing the winner to claim the reward. It should be noted that, as in people, generalizations about crow behavior cannot be inferred across the board. Differences in food sharing can change depending on location and the established customs of a particular group of crows.

Although I had never witnessed the W's actually catch a field mouse, I believe I saw them hunting from the telephone wires above the railroad tracks. They would stare intently at the ground below, then swiftly swoop down, hawklike. As my view was obscured by foliage, I could only infer that the swooping crow had spied a small rodent and, taking advantage of the moment, tried to grab him for a meal. In fact, a few years before I began studying the W family of crows, I heard the sound of a creature in distress coming from the neighbor's yard. Following my ears, I looked up and saw a crow in the tree above me, holding a baby cottontail by the ears. As I watched, the crow secured the rabbit on the stout branch, and began hammering it on the head with machine-gun rhythm. The rabbit screamed for its life, and I, sickened by its distress, made a move and a sound to scare the crow into dropping it, hoping the fall would shorten its suffering. I was neither taking sides in this battle nor begrudging anyone a meal; I just wanted to interfere long enough to bring a swift end to this rabbit's pleas for mercy. The crow released the rabbit, but the baby—although it landed with one hard bounce and a roll—survived, much to my dismay. Even if it could escape the crow's supper table for the day, I wasn't sure it could survive and enjoy a normal life. Adding to the grim scene was the sight of the mother rabbit trying now to shoo the stunned baby into the safety of the tangle of perennials under a birdbath. The outcome of this saga I will never know, as when I checked the scene later, order had once again been restored to the idyllic garden, as though no life-and-death drama had ever unfolded there.

The crows kept a regular visiting schedule, arriving in the morning at first light. Many times, one of them would fly over the house while I was still in bed, making a distinctive call that I felt was related to marking territory. I thought perhaps Winona performed this task. Invisible lines seemed to designate different groups' territories, and the crows surely understood where their territories began and ended. I could not follow the W's beyond certain points, but within the small range that I was able to observe them, I began to understand these invisible lines also. The second group of crows I became aware of hung around to the south of the W family. They occupied and defended the school field and the south section of the W's park. On one of my first explorations into this territory, I encountered a group of four or more crows perched in the trees lining the school field. I did not know upon my approach if these might be the W's, nor did I understand the relationship between the two groups. As I passed under their perches, these crows began to scream at me as if I were a terrible monster, and they were alerting my intrusion to anyone who would listen. I dropped a pile of nuts for this group, but they stared at them blankly, even after I retreated to a safe distance. These were surely not the W's.

I sometimes spotted members of this second group of crows perched on the telephone pole at the far end of the block, to the east of the garage roof. Their sharp vision, I'm sure, allowed them to see me feeding the W family there, but they were never included in this feeding frenzy. In fact, Willy and Wilbur chased them vigorously when they tried to approach the piles of food. These flights were not casual, floating forays, but the flights of black darts flying with the speed of bullets and sounding angry caws at the intruders.

As the days of December darkened and outdoor sources of food became more limited, this second group of crows became bolder in its attempts to partake in the bounty on the roof. The beginnings of a territory war erupted literally over my very head. When I had begun feeding and befriending the W family, this other group had stayed happily on the periphery, not disputing the line that probably had existed peacefully between the groups for some time. Things began to change when the W's territory became desirable to the other group. Much like housing values when a neighborhood becomes either more attractive or more rundown, the territory that included my garage roof was in a state of flux.

I needed a name to identify the second group of crows. At first I did not know if they were a family group or just a motley collection of unrelated birds. They certainly looked the part of a ragtag team of vagabonds, with their tattered plumage and scrappy behaviors. A feisty group, whose leader was a rumpled bird with a distinctive smoker's rasp to his caw and whitish, crusty patches over both elbows, as though he were wearing an old sweater. I suspected some form of ectoparasite—that had taken up residence and stubbornly refused to leave—had caused the patches. The word "scrap" seemed to fit what seemed a conglomerate of unmatched pieces of family, either older birds who had lost their mates or youngsters not ready to strike out on their own. I decided to call them the Scraps. Although I would normally be rooting for the underdog in such a fight, I couldn't feel the same allegiance toward the Scraps as I did toward the W's. Still, I respected them.

After the Scraps discovered the magic of the roof, they opposed the W family regularly—even though they never dared alight on the garage roof to steal food. It was as though they were fighting for the right to do so. There were skirmishes in the air, during which two birds wrestled, momentarily grasping at the other with outstretched feet or poking aggressively midair with a beak. There was also the aforementioned aggressive chasing, mostly on the part of the W's. Each morning began with a war of caws between the two factions.

It was a slice of pecan pie that finally tempted one of the Scraps to swoop in. I like pecan pie. Crows like pecan pie. And when I buy my pie from a grocery store rather than from a high-end bakery, there is sure to be pie left over. The Scrap swooped in and stole this forbidden morsel from the roof in a swift and gutsy move. He then flew directly to a roof in his territory and placed the slice of pie neatly and deliberately on top of a metal chimney cover. Wilbur and Willy were incensed and sprang from their perches to dive-bomb the Scraps. There were aerial wrestling matches followed by a return to prominent perches, from which insults were screamed. The W's treated the theft as a high offense. Winona stayed put on the light post, joining in the excited, hysterical chorus of cawing, while Wilbur and Willy made repeated missions to the other side.

This flying and fighting went on for about five minutes before Winona got a bright idea. Gracefully, quietly, she flew to the pie unnoticed and retrieved it, carrying it to the area near the railroad tracks. During this conflict, I began to understand that the pie had become secondary to the conflict over territory. Wilbur and Willy went on grappling with the Scraps for several minutes before everyone noticed the pie was gone. The solution was pure Winona; she is observant, unemotional, and clever.

A little further into the season, a midwinter cold snap overtook us, and the ground was covered in snow too deep for crows to forage in. I shoveled a little patch in the back garden and retrained the crows to come there for food. They were reluctant at first, as with all new things, but I let hunger and pizza convince them. Willy was often brave enough to stroll up to the back gate and peer through the slats into the rest of the yard. It gave me a thrill to see the W's land on the ground closer than they had ever been to the house. I loved to go out after they had gone to study their delicate tracks in the light dusting of snow.

The days were cold and short, and, with the ground frozen and snow covered, I thought about how tough it must have been for the Scrap family to find food. Because of my help, the W's were not finding times as hard. One day I put out leftover chili. The W's ate some of it then perched on a wire over the yard. Suddenly, all three began to call in the direction of the Scraps. It was not the usual aggressive call I had heard them use to mark their territory but more like the call they used to attract each other's attention. I had heard Winona use this call to let her family know when breakfast was on, and now all three were calling this way in unison. Were they inviting the Scraps over to share their meal? Could crows realize another group's predicament and be willing to help them? Had the Scraps somehow communicated with the W's their need for food? Would severe weather or other hardship make separate groups of crows more generous toward each other and willing to share a surplus?

As I pondered these questions, the Scraps flew over to my yard and took some of the chili. The W's did not appear to mind, as they did not harass the Scraps in the usual way. It appeared to me that they had invited their neighbors over for a meal. This heartwarming tale might make for a Hallmark Classic were it not for the tiny detail I left out of the story. Before sending their invitation, the W's had carefully picked all of the meat out of the chili, leaving only beans and sauce for the Scraps. I guess even a crow's generosity has its limits.

My life and routine had become entwined with the crows—starting in the morning when I fed them and including my afternoon walk to the park. Their voices outside brought me to the window, and I watched for them in spare moments. I loved them as much as if they had been pets living in my home. I am quite sure they loved me, too. I could see it in the way they looked at me and the way they trusted me within arm's reach. I could see it in the quizzical and astonished looks of passersby as they watched the crows swirl over me in greeting or creep within feet of me as I sat waiting patiently in the grass. No stranger could do what I was doing. I had pierced the veil of wildness in them—just enough to love them but not enough to tame them. Our relationship was an equal mix of admiration, respect, and familiarity.

In a modern urban setting, it is easy to lose touch with the natural world to which we all belong. These crows brought me to a place of long ago, when humans watched the signs in the heavens with more wonder than knowledge. These people did not understand the workings of the earth in technical terms, but they could read the signs with their hearts and senses. This is how it feels to connect with wild crows. Looking up into the bright sky, I could smell the sunshine on their feathers and know their minds with my soul. It is like a song, which is cryptic as notes written on paper but makes perfect sense played on the guitar. A crow's love is like a wisp of smoke: one moment there, and the next, something too slippery to explain.

Humans have always sought to befriend wild creatures, from tourists feeding bears in Yellowstone to birders providing seed for songbirds. In some instances, as with the bears in Yellowstone, such practices have led to disaster. The large, fierce bears adapted too well to the handouts, causing damage to property and other unwanted consequences. Efforts to reduce their dependence on humans have only recently begun to pay off. Wildlife biologists have concluded that it is easier to train one bear to stay away from people than to educate the many well-meaning souls with a lunch to share and a desire to see a bear up close.

I do not hold myself above the masses or feel entitled to turn a small crow population into a pesky bunch of freeloaders, pounding on strangers' garage roofs demanding peanuts, or buzzing over people's heads in what they view as a friendly hello. I was glad to find, therefore, that the crows I came to know did not generalize their views about all people. They were just as wary of strangers as they had always been. In fact, there were times when I walked to the park with a friend, and they refused to approach me because they did not trust the stranger who was with me.

5

Roosts

In my area, winter roosts began forming right after Thanksgiving. Crows from every direction gathered in huge groups to sleep in predesignated areas. I wondered where my own group slept and studied the map for clues. What might draw them to fly off to bed in the same direction every evening? Using their arrival time in the morning as a measure, I guessed that wherever the roost was, it wasn't more than a half-hour flight, assuming they did not leave before dawn. Birds can and do fly at night, especially in cities where lights from below can be used to help them navigate. Estimates suggest that crows fly up to fifty miles each day between roost and home range.

As dusk approached, the W's perched on the wires above the railroad tracks. Soon, one of them would give the signal that spurred the others to follow. Sometimes as I watched from the house or yard, it was Winona, her body contorting and bouncing—the motion that at a soundless distance I knew was her staccato cawing. She would turn swiftly and on rapid wingbeat lead the boys to roost. At other times, it would be Wilbur, who, without any verbal warning, would suddenly decide it was time to go. Silently his family would retreat to their private place. The pattern of leaving was as varied as the changing weather. As quickly as I could make an assumption, another day would prove me wrong. The three, not always of one mind, would often disagree as to when to end a day, and one of them would linger after the others had left. But always, as I watched the black dots disappear in the dimming light, I was confident of their morning return.

On any gray winter afternoon, crows begin their daily journey: hundreds of the black birds stream across the dismal backdrop, flying to their roost for sleep and camaraderie. One theory says that crows in this way share lucrative forage areas in times of food shortage. Others cite protection from predators, warmth from city lights, and social opportunities. Whatever advantages these roosts provided, the daily exodus was a sight not to be missed by any crow lover.

Although curious and anxious to witness a roost myself, I never was able to locate one on my own. It was only by luck and an overheard conversation that I found myself traveling to the location of my first roost. As a result of my years of searching for relevant information, I had begun to envision a spot in some exotic place. Imagine my surprise when, while conversing with a customer in the town in which I had worked every day for the past fifteen years, a casual observer informed me that I was standing in a building squarely in the midst of a giant crow roost! Feeling there must be some mistake, I quizzed him for details. His replies convinced me to check out this information with more expectation than skepticism.

It seemed the crows at this particular roost occupied several favored spots, which now, armed with a map, I was privy to. Subsequent investigation showed that a surprisingly high number of college campuses are preferred roosting sites. The roost I found was no exception, as part of it spanned the campus of a noted university, expanding into the outskirts of the downtown and a park bordered by a lake.

I timed my arrival for after dark, assuming the birds would be settled by then. Stopped at a traffic light downtown, I craned my neck to peer through the windshield and was delighted to see a group of fifteen or more birds gathered above me in the limbs of a tree. Even more excited, I searched for a place to park.

Once out of the car and on foot, I hurried toward a small grove of trees that was set back from the street, a few steps below street level. A bronze statue of a seated man gazed tenderly at a child in his lap, while above, a triple-digit murder of crows perched in plain view.

My first awareness was of the cacophony of sound. The noise was a mix of rattles, squawks, and caws, giving the impression of many conversations taking place at once. Not the usual long distance calls, these intimate sounds took on a different tenor. They were voiced quickly, with a variation of enunciation and vowel-like mutterings. I looked into the faces of those passing on the street, incredulous that they were not looking above them to see what was causing this racket. Lost in thought or oblivious to their surroundings, they were missing a stunning show of nature in the heart of the city. I wanted to rush up, shake their shoulders, and shout, "Isn't this the coolest thing you've ever seen?" Instead, I stood silently taking it all in and trying to comprehend its meaning.

A few of the birds were dozing, but it was obviously much too early in the evening to call it quits for Corvids of such a social nature. The crows changed seats frequently, alluding to their individual preferences. But the main characteristic of this group was cohesiveness. This marked the first time I had ever witnessed flocking behavior in crows, as the small groups I observed at home lived in families, quite clearly acting as individual minds. This roosting bunch startled easily and flew as a unified group, surrendering their separateness for the safety of the whole.

The sound of their many wings and the sight of these birds known to me so personally acting on behalf of a greater good gave me insight into an aspect of crows that had previously been hidden from me. I saw what farmers saw—a mindless cadre without personality. This flocking diminished the individual bird somehow, giving the impression that it could not survive without the bulk of numbers, although this impression was contrary to my own experiences. Still, this flock reminded me of ants swarming over a cookie. Illusion or not, I realized it was all some people knew of crows.

Return visits to this site over the next few weeks revealed that the crows were rarely predictable in their choice of spots for the night. One late afternoon in December I found them dodging wet snowflakes as they foraged on the ground in a large park near the lake. Several hundred birds dotted the surrounding trees in a tightly woven circle. I peered through the window of my car, straining past the distortions of wet glass to watch the birds as they prepared for night. Many were on the ground, walking in aimless, winding paths, sometimes stopping to caw. Still others stood on the ground quietly, not moving at all, waiting for who knows what. Above, in the trees, crows swayed like rocking chairs while holding their wings slightly away from their bodies—the posture of the cawing bird. A group of three crows, high above me, worked on what appeared to be a former nest. Whether this was a serious endeavor or just playing at the future, I do not know. One bird ripped at small twigs, while another, squatting in the nest, seemed busy weaving. Was this their nest from the previous year? Was it even a crow's nest? Were they making a meal of broken eggshells?

As dusk dimmed even further, ending the day, smaller factions of thirty or more crows branched off from this main grouping, presumably to find their own niches. Researchers studying radio-tagged crows have not found any indication that families stay together at the roost. Various spots in town are resting places for crows, and it appears they change positions throughout the night much like a sleeper who tosses and turns, looking for the most comfortable spot. In the crows' case, they may move because a sight or sound disturbed them, causing them to fly off en masse to another location a few blocks or trees away.

The terrain of the roosting area I had discovered varied greatly. The roosting choices included brightly lit stores and eateries, lakefront parks, buildings on the university campus, and old-growth trees downtown settled in among the office buildings made of reflective glass. One preferred roosting tree placed the birds in full view of the condominium on the corner across from the Whole Foods Market. The entire expanse of the area was not more than two square miles. Smaller groups of crows broke away and fanned out to cover the distance like cliques of schoolchildren clustered together on a playground. Most of the roosting spots I located were lit by the purple glow of winter streetlights, making enemies more visible to those crows charged with sentry duty.

By day, it was convenient for me to check which trees were favorites for roosting—evidence was easy to find in the form of white splotching below. During one such investigation I discovered a dehydrated crow carcass, feathers, and beak still attached. The noontime lunch crowd stepped over it, hurrying to get a bite. It appeared that an owl or hawk had had the same idea; however, his appetite had propelled him not toward the Subway sandwich shop but toward the congregation of crows.

It was never very hard for me to find the roost once I arrived in town. I cast my gaze toward the sky and followed the dotted black arrow of crows. Determined to approximate the number of their roost, I trailed a group one frigid January afternoon. They led me to a sandy beach bounded by a snow fence and a stand of bare-limbed trees. Crossing the busy road to get closer to them, I was transported to another world. Here, against the pastel blue-pink sky, the snow-covered sand, and the frigid waters, hundreds of crows milled about as though engaged in a summer picnic. The sheer beauty of the scene made me giddy. I laughed aloud involuntarily and snapped picture after picture, forever saving the moment. Oblivious to the cold, I attempted to count the moving objects, finally estimating groups of ten and extrapolating the final figure. Based on the photographs I used later to check my calculations, I determined that this roost flock was made up of between three and four hundred birds. Not huge by other documented standards, but large enough to cause the complaint of the local people who must step over the spotted mess in the morning.

One kindly soul, a worker in one of the crows' favorite buildings, washed down the walkways first thing each morning before the tenants arrived for work. Such duties are his job, but I suspect that he also does it, as fellow crow lover, because he doesn't want the birds banished by those on the top floors capable of making such decisions.

I continued my winter pilgrimages to see the roosting crows, hoping for new insights and enjoying the splendid sights and sounds of such a large congregation. During these times my thoughts always strayed to my own crow friends. I wondered if they might spot me here and venture forth to help me solve a small piece of the mystery of their daily lives.

6

The Hunted and the Hated

Any writing on crows would be disingenuous if it did not acknowledge the fact that many people detest them. Some blindly follow a tradition of hatred without giving it much thought. Some people witness events that sour their feelings, such as a crow robbing a songbird's nest in the garden. To many people, crows' large winter roosts are yet another source of annoyance. These large congregations can cause consternation for those who must walk over areas soiled by bird droppings in order to get into their houses or office buildings. Yet others believe crows' harsh voices are synonymous with cruel personalities.

The most vitriolic feelings about the birds seem reserved for the crow hunter. Killing these birds for sport, some people do not even bother to hide their blood thirst behind lofty ideals. Reading excerpts from a Web site devoted to the crow hunter—like eavesdropping on a private conversation—reveals feelings that might be masked in mixed company. I visited the site Crowbusters.com, and, after I had gathered the courage to sift through some of the abhorrent rhetoric, I learned a few things—not only about the darker side of human nature but about the hunters' vast field experience and knowledge of the crow.

The site featured pictures as well as stories. In one picture, camouflaged men stood proudly before hundreds of dead birds, lined up at perfect intervals in a mosaic pattern. In others, young boys, smiling gleefully, held up their fresh kills for the admiring audience behind the camera. One-of-a-kind specimens—all-gray birds, pure white specimens, and the pied crow—were prominently featured on the Web site.

I explored the minds of the hunters themselves, examining their thoughts as expressed on the bulletin board. Many sought advice on the best techniques to kill more birds or bragged like fisherman back from the sea. In some, I found their cruelty toward living creatures only thinly veiled. Some of the hunters even advocated using maimed crows as decoys, the cries of which would draw in the crow's comrades, who would thus become prey for the men lying in wait.

Another idea was to obtain a crow too young to feed itself, and wean it to a pan of dog food set out next to it. This was supposed to be a taming process. Once the taming was accomplished, it would be easy to attach a plastic band to the crow's leg. This would provide convenient collar for a leash made of string and secured to a tree limb. Now the crow could—"turn on its relatives" by "calling madly"—when ever they approached.

Although people claim to hunt crows for various reasons—ranging from their intelligence and worthy-opponent status to environmental depredation caused by their feeding habits—some hunters' unabashed glee at killing seeps from between the lines of their writings.

One hunter watched a pair of crows fly over his house and wondered about the coloration of the head of one bird. It reminded him of an "eagle head snow goose." Instead of marveling at the wonder, or better still checking a field guide to see if such a bird actually existed, he hoped it would hang around the area long enough for him to give it a dose of "lead poisoning." It scared me to think there were men with guns shooting at birds they had not properly identified, much less at Wilbur's descendents.

Most of the crow hunters were thrilled at killing the birds and reported of the "goose bumps" they got when they thought about how many crows they "hammered" in one session.

Another hunter rationalized his killing with his own interpretation of a "murder" of crows. He felt they had no mercy on their victims—sighting the oft-repeated predation of young songbirds—and added his own twist with vivid descriptions of their malevolent hearts as they tore into still live prey, and ripped it to pieces for their young. Adding his observation that they will attack a newborn calf before it can walk in order to peck the eyes for a meal.

This hunter's inaccurate conclusions only served to cloud things further. It is virtually impossible for a crow to damage a calf's eye in this way, much less eat it. In most vertebrates, a tough covering protects this delicate structure from injury.

While evil intent is projected onto the crow responsible for the actions described above, the bird is only looking to eat or feed its young. It does not take the young nestlings to punish them for some perceived wrongdoing. How then does the hunter reconcile his vengeance toward the crow? Would he be as willing to take his punishment from the relatives of the cows, pigs, chickens, and other assorted beings he has eaten in his lifetime?

Still another justification for shooting crows referenced historic battlefields and the image of crows "picking the bones" of "fallen soldiers." The hunter imagined himself the victim of this practice should his "carcass" be left outdoors. "It makes crow shooting more satisfying," he concluded.

Those who express anti-hunting opinions on this Web site are ridiculed in a section reserved for hate mail. As I read through the observations and sarcastic responses, I remembered the feelings evoked by the bullies on the playground in elementary school, who, when they are finally shouted down by those who disagree with their brutality, laugh with wicked satisfaction at having provoked the sensitive weaklings. Perhaps at the root of their killing frenzy lies a desire to destroy that which they will never possess. The spirit of the kind and gentle seems beyond their grasp; the crows' true connection to the earth and the peaceful joy it brings to those who understand seem, to them, a vile envy.

More than one person beseeched the hunters for advice on getting rid of the nuisance they found so intolerable. Fueled by the belief that the crows that made a "huge noise" outside their home deserved to be killed, they asked for advice on how to accomplish this without a gun. The "little black bastard" had increased too rapidly for their liking they complained.

The people of Auburn, New York, have stirred up controversy by establishing an annual shooting event aimed at ridding the town of roosting crows. Auburn is home to one of the largest winter roosts in the country, and folks there square off over what course of action to take, as once again humans try to control nature in accordance with their own plans. Crow hunters are only too happy to oblige the faction in Auburn who wishes to annihilate the crows, turning the outskirts of the town into a crow-killing extravaganza complete with prizes for the team that kills the most birds. Mirroring the Internet Web site's tone, jokes are made of the protesters' objections to this slaughter. A local bar serves deep-fried crow sand-wiches, and crow hunters wear T-shirts emblazoned with "Beer-guzzling Gomer," mocking the insults hurled by the Corvid-loving public.

As long as crows and people inhabit the same planet, this disagreement will play out—along with the multitude of other dramas puzzling to those of us who care for the earth and the creatures that live on it. As humans, we sometimes fail to look at the bigger picture, to see our own hand in the environmental clashes between humans and the creatures with which we share the earth.

7

Mysteries of the Nest

Like all good friends who have known each other awhile, the W family and I fell into a steady pattern of interaction. They hadn't surprised me for some time. There were times I pondered our inability to take the next step forward, whatever that may have been. Could I, for example, coax them to take food from my hand the way some tame chickadees did? It was while in this state of mind that I began to notice subtle changes in the crows' day-to-day activities. It didn't register at first when they missed a day here or there in the morning. I assumed they were just occupied with crow business. The food was always gone from the roof when I came home, so perhaps they were sleeping in and collecting the groceries later than usual. Then I noticed that they seemed less hungry, less enthusiastic about the food.

Many times, it was Winona I would see while I was getting ready to leave for work. She would sit over the roof, without taking any food, and call for the boys a long time. Her patience wearing into urgency, she cawed toward the far end of the park. It was there that I had seen Wilbur and Willy flying, drawn as if by some unseen magnet. Winona was often still perched on the wire as I left for work. "Why won't you take some food for yourself at least?" I asked. She flinched involuntarily at the sound of my whisper. Easily spooked by humans, she tolerated my inquiry, but gave no reply.

I began watching the mornings with increasing wonder and a bit of worry as I grappled with the possible cause of this new pattern. Food seemed to have become secondary to the secret pursuit shared by Wilbur and Willy. A few times when they had settled in to pick at the pizza crusts on the roof, they were summoned by this force mid-meal and took off flying toward the far end of the park, neither finishing the scraps nor returning for them later. I took detours on my way to work, driving around the park looking for the giant crow Mecca that pulled them away from me. But I only came away puzzled.

The starlings were starting to notice the pattern also, and they began to take advantage of it, finishing all my crow offerings like starving piranhas. Now I worried that, even if the crows were returning later, there would be nothing left for them. I was troubled. If it weren't for the regularity of the afternoon walks the W's still took with my dog and me, I would have been despondent over the changes I was seeing in the mornings.

Then it happened. The crows began acting strangely toward me. They ignored me. It was as though they didn't know me. They stopped their morning visits completely. I was heartbroken. Had I done something to lose their trust? Had I accidentally fed them something that had made them sick? At times, I even wondered if they were the same crows. I whistled to them from the park as they sat on the wires over the railroad tracks, but they pretended not to hear me. In the past, they had never needed any prompt to come flying over to greet me.

I made excuses in my head for their behavior, like a rejected lover, not able to take in the thought that our special relationship may have been some fluke. Had it been a short but beautiful dream that had now abruptly ended? Although I still saw them in the afternoons, they didn't come to the park while I was there. They sat passively over the railroad tracks, and I could no longer be sure they even recognized me. Occasionally one of the crows would break free of the others and fly over to steal a nut from me. But something was wrong. The two left behind protested this action loudly, and I got the feeling a rule had been broken. But I still couldn't allow it to sink in.

What had happened to my crows? It was late February, and I wondered if they could be starting their breeding and nesting cycle. If so, was it possibly causing them to act this way? I read my crow reference books repeatedly, clinging to one sentence here or there about how secretive crows become during breeding season. But I did not understand why this state of affairs should alter our relationship. Perhaps the drive to keep their future offspring safe had caused them to become elusive and single-minded. Could hormonal changes be guiding their behavior? I hoped it was only a phase and that time would bring them back to me, but doubt crept into my mind at every turn. I ruminated about unknowingly having broken a sacred trust.

Some days can be among the saddest you will face, and yet you don't know it until later on—like the day you say good-bye to a friend without knowing it will be the last time you see him. Maybe he knows it but can't tell you. Like if he's a crow. Just before the crows stopped their visits and started ignoring me, Willy did some unusual things. When I theorized that the crows might be starting their nesting season, I thought his behavior might be due to feeling left out. I assumed he would have a secondary role as helper at the nest. With his parents busy with other concerns, he often showed up alone. He sat on the fence by the railroad, picking at the dried vines as though he were lonely and looking for a way to amuse himself. Once as I was walking the dog, he called out to me in a tone I can only describe as forlorn. It was a warbled lament. I had never heard a crow make a sound like that before. I looked around for another crow he might be talking to, but I was the only other crow around. He seemed to be talking to me. But I didn't figure out the message until many months later. Willy knew he was leaving to start a new life, but I didn't.

He knew it on the Saturday I watched him in my neighbor's yard from the front window of my house. I got my binoculars for a closer look. Having done earlier tests, I knew the crows could see me through the glass. There were candidate signs for an upcoming election stuck in my neighbor's lawn, and Willy made me laugh as he strolled up to each one of them, as if carefully reading the text. He seemed to study the faces of the people pictured on the signs as though he could tell their characters from the lines around their eyes. He was walking right toward me, closer and closer and closer, until the binoculars went out of focus, and I had to put them down. Suddenly he flew up to my porch railing and landed! The crows had never ventured this close to me before. I was less than three feet from Willy on the other side of the window.

He calmly looked at me for the longest time, as if finally giving me what I had wanted most. I could see every detail of his feathering, as though looking at a photograph in a book. I could see the true coloring of his eyes, which were brown and not black, as they had seemed from a distance. I had never seen a crow at such close range, and the experience was both stunning and paralyzing. I didn't know what to do. Perhaps Willy was having the same thoughts about me, this human he had come to know more intimately than he had ever known a creature from another species. I didn't know Willy was saying good-bye.

He spent several spellbinding minutes with me before he flew away. But before he did, he quite deliberately pooped right on my porch. I know it sounds crazy, but knowing what I do now about that event, I think of it as if he were symbolically leaving something of himself behind. Even as the white stain faded away, his memory remained vivid in my heart.

The W's were gone. It was as if they had never existed. I no longer even saw them in the distance, ignoring me. I scanned the sky constantly, looking for some sign that they were still alive. I was tortured by thoughts of them attacked by hawks, their heads torn from their bodies and eaten. I would have traded the privilege of having ever known them for one more glimpse to know that they were all right. I was as surprised by their disappearance as I had been by their strange reactions to me in the days that preceded it.

I picked at my lunch one day, knowing it would be useless to save any left-overs for the crows that no longer shared my life. I noticed the mornings were deadly quiet and devoid of cawing. Even the Scrap family was silent. I took heart one day at the sight of a crow carrying a stick in a neighborhood near my own. It was a sign that other crows were nesting, and it kept my hopes alive. I was still putting out nuts in the mornings, although I had discontinued the variable feasts I had once provided. I did so mostly out of courtesy to the blue jays, but if my crows did return some day, I didn't want them to think I had forgotten them.

In the moments buoyed by hope that the W's had left the area only to make their nest, I calculated the amount of time needed to complete their task and return to me. It takes twelve days to build a crow's nest. Crow eggs are incubated for approximately eighteen days. Four to six eggs are usually laid. Only two of these small crows survive to see their first year. Baby crows leave the nest about thirty-five days after hatching, but they continue to be cared for by adult mem-bers of the family. Some young crows disperse as early as the fall of their first year, joining large aggregate flocks, while others stick close to home for up to six years.

The days became warmer, and I spent weekends trekking around the area looking for signs of my errant crows. Perhaps, with a combination of luck and sore feet, I would stumble upon their nest. I quickly learned that trees in the dis-tance to which I had seen the W's fly—while appearing only blocks away from my front window—are actually miles away. And they are mostly impossible to find from the perspective of the ground. No longer able to rely on visual cues, I became lost in a sea of tree trunks and car traffic. I longed to fly, my heart soaring at the thought of being able to follow my crows, at finally solving the mysteries of their existence.

After my luckless forays into the wilds of the city, I was uncomfortably lonely for the company of Corvids. My sheltie and I expanded our daily walks to the far end of the park, where I had seen foreign crows in the past. Anxious to cultivate any crow friends and to scan their faces for any sign of the W's I fought the fluc-tuating weather of early spring—one day pelted by an icy rain and the next shar-ing the sun with the songs of white-throated sparrows winging toward their summer grounds.

I was happy to find a gang of rowdy crows cawing angrily as I passed under their high perches at the very end of the park. I could tell that they had haunted the area for some time by the white splotches on the park benches and the many black feathers scattered on the ground. It was a sad experience after all I had known to be disliked so by this pack. I was used to an affectionate welcome, but this group regarded me as an intruding human, no more useful than the passing high school students whooping loudly to scare them off.

I pulled a large pile of unsalted peanuts from my jean jacket and placed them carefully on a bare patch of ground, watched all the while being by several pairs of suspicious eyes. I turned and left quickly, not even daring to watch to see if the wary crows would take my peace offering. They would figure it out, and I would be back tomorrow.

Back in the garden, the Scrap family has become emboldened by the home group's absence. They may have even known exactly where the W's were. Did they also know the W's would never return? Perhaps I was incorrect in thinking they had left only to build their nest. Maybe some unseen battle had ensued, and the Scraps were the victors. They did outnumber the W's by one member. And why weren't the Scraps off building their own nest? Instead, they were hanging around my garden, sneaking the nuts I put out for the blue jays, unaware that I was watching them from inside my kitchen. Soon they had taken over the W's old habit of waiting in the morning for me to put out their breakfast. The Scraps were nowhere near as friendly as the W's. I felt used by them and resentful that they had usurped my beloved W family's position. But they were crows after all, and I wondered if I would have to adjust to the fact that they had taken over the territory for good.

One thing seemed apparent: they had been observing the W's carefully from a distance and began to mimic some of their behaviors. One crow that seemed bolder than the rest began sitting on the telephone wire, waiting for me to notice him. He seemed to be thinking, "Well, this is how Wilbur did it." I did notice him and tried to encourage his confidence by approaching and rewarding him with treats in the same cautious way I had back in the beginning. I hated starting over.

After a few weeks, this crow began to accept my presence. I could pick him out from the bunch, mostly because of the white, crusty patches on his elbows, but also because of his distinctive caw. It sounded as though he was hoarse. Was his strange voice related to his run-down condition? The crusts on his elbows were, after all, not a sign of good health. My avian vet confirmed my suspicion that they were probably ectoparasites as she patiently looked over the stack of crow photos I had brought to show her.

It was also possible he was a transplanted crow who had picked up the dialect of the crows somewhere far from here. Birds are known to develop local dialects.

Even the crows I hear a few miles away, near the lake, have a slightly different accent.

I had heard this crow previously and recognized him as the caller who seemed to announce my arrivals home to the neighborhood. I began to suspect this occurrence over the winter when, walking from the garage after work, I would hear the same crow's raspy voice alerting everyone to my presence. I wondered for a while if he might be doing his neighbors the W's a favor. "Wilbur, your girl is home," he seemed to chime, but I dismissed the notion as silly and egocentric. Still it became more than coincidence to hear this crow every day as I walked up the steps to the back door.

A name for this crow came to me easily, as he triggered memories of another favorite childhood book, *The Yearling*. I called him Fodderwing, after the character with whom he shared a bit of a physical challenge. As Fodderwing warmed to me, he sometimes ventured onto the roof in my presence. Although still somewhat wary, he seemed to have a sense of humor, once playing what I interpreted as a crow joke on me. When I came outside to feed him, he was sitting on the wire, next to a large transformer. This large square box was near the telephone pole. When he saw me, he ducked behind it, as if to hide but then, like a small child learning about object permanence, peeked out at me again with a mischievous glint in his eye.

I decided I could like Fodderwing without betraying my loyalty to Wilbur and the other W's. And as the feelings became mutual, Fodderwing began to bring a friend along for his morning vigil on the line. I called this crow Spook, because the minute he saw me, he flew off, cawing with agitation, as though my proximity was too much to bear. I saw these two with regularity now, and as the days warmed up I began to eat my meals on the deck. Fodderwing watched me from his seat on the telephone pole, seeming to wonder if I would save him a bite. When I did, he rewarded me by coming to the roof without hesitation. It seemed I had won his friendship.

It was early May, and the warm days allowed me to become more familiar with the Scraps. I wondered what had brought these four together—were they a family unit like the W's or some other conglomerate of relations? They could have been several young birds not yet paired off for breeding. I based this assumption on the fact that they were not acting strangely skittish toward me or secretive in their actions, like nesting crows. In fact, it was just the opposite; they were slowly becoming tamer.

Conversely, evidence that Fodderwing was nesting was manifested by his intense interest in hunting baby rabbits. Since rabbit meat makes up the major portion of a young crow's diet, this behavior led me to believe there were Scrap youngsters to feed. Fodderwing and another unidentified crow had been persistently watching a nest of rabbits they had discovered on the green space adjacent to the railroad tracks. This hunting made the crows intensely serious. They spent hypnotic spans of time, keen to detect the movement of young below, hunched over pertinent places, waiting for an opportune moment to strike.

I discovered another rabbits' nest in the neighbor's garden, next to my own garage, keeping the crows vigilant there as well. This led to a surprise encounter one rainy morning as I left for work. Hearing cawing, I opened the overhead door, wanting to see where it was coming from, when suddenly one of the Scraps landed not two feet from me on the neighbor's fence. So absorbed was he in the moment and lost in the possibility of catching one of the elusive rabbits, he did not even notice me at first. When his spell of concentration was finally broken, he startled at my nearness and flew off with a burst of adrenaline at having been so close to a human. It gave me a rush also. I found it curious that the Scraps—if in fact they were tending a nest—had not lost their appetite for my cooking, nor had they become skittish in their roof visits, leading me to question once again the reasons behind the W's puzzling departure. There was so much to ponder about crows, and so few ways to find out the reasons for their actions.

After a long stretch of rain, the large mud puddle that always forms in the park was at high tide. A duck was camped out there, catching my interest. Then I noticed the crow in the W's old haunt, fishing around in the wet earth, looking for worms. Could it be they had returned? I dashed back to the house to get some leftover pork and ran to the park. The crow ruffled and shook his feathers when he saw me. As though recognizing a friend, he flew toward me to a tree. I was almost sure it was Wilbur. "Crow," I called out and whistled, but he was nervous and flew to a higher branch. I dropped the meat, and backed away, watching. He dropped to the ground, confiscated the meat, and flew with it to the factory roof.

I was watching the crow tear up the meat I had given him, when another crow, whom I assumed to be Winona, appeared on the roof. She stretched herself thin, raising her head and straining to see me in the distance. For a moment, she allowed herself this distraction but then quickly turned back to the life she had been pursuing without me. Ignoring me once again, she shared the meat with Wilbur. I stayed watching for as long as they remained, but neither returned to the park or acknowledged me before flying off in the direction that held the mystery of their universe.

This short visit gave me hope and relief. I now knew the W's had not perished as my imaginings had led me to fear. But I was also disappointed that the crows had not appeared to share my intense feelings at the brief reunion. Upon reflection, I took into account the impossibility of reading a bird's mind. After all, I couldn't be sure that they were not drawn back here by a desire to check in with a friend. Whatever had taken them away from me occupied their attention and called them back. My faith was renewed that whatever spell they were under could be broken. This was what I chose to believe as days passed with no repeat visits.

Meanwhile, I visited the far end of the park, cultivating my relationships there with daily nut offerings. The crows recognized me now and no longer shouted angrily as I approached. To the contrary, they welcomed my visits and sometimes posted a scout who called to the other crows at my approach. I could sit quietly at a distance, tossing nuts under trees at convenient spots for my new group of friends. It was exciting to have made this progress, and I took pride in my abilities to win over strange groups of crows in such record time.

I suspected I had some help, however, from a crow who seemed especially familiar with me, even though I did not recognize him. He seemed to have accepted me more quickly than the others and at times even followed me home, begging nuts on the way, but he always stopped short of the park maintenance house, which, I concluded, marked the edge of his group's territory. This crow's acceptance caused the others to trust me more rapidly, in the same way humans welcome strangers much more readily when mutual friends introduce them. The only explanation I had for this situation was that he must have been a member of the Scrap family. It made me curious about cooperative relationships between neighboring crows. Why would this crow be accepted into another family? I was grateful for his assistance.

This group in the park seemed to be cohesive and larger than either the W's or the Scraps. It was hard to know how many there were, because on any given day their numbers fluctuated. There seemed to be five to seven birds in this bunch I now called the Parkers. Not long after the Parkers become more comfortable with me, I was treated to the first forays of some of the newly fledged baby Parkers. I placed the nuts on a park bench and retreated to watch. It didn't take long for the first crow to alight, and once he did, many more pushed their way to the center of the pile to get one. A baby begged his elder for a nut and was rebuffed. The parent must teach the baby what to eat but after a time stop feeding him, even though he may continue to beg. The young crow was probably only about six weeks old and still quite clumsy. He tried his luck on his own nut, but he was not sure how to crack it and gave up. Learning quickly, he picked up the scrap pieces left by the other crows and examined the empty hulls carefully. Another of his siblings with more experience was able to crack his own nuts and busily eats the fruit of his labor. He had probably had some practice on a nut his parent presented to him to play with, and I was certain his fledge mate wouldn't be too far behind in nut-cracking school.

After the group had finished the pile of nuts and was loitering either on the ground or just above in the trees, I slowly walked back toward them, confident that they were losing their fear of me. But this time they fled and screamed at me again, as though I had dropped in rank to stranger. It struck me that they were more cautious because of the young crows, perhaps because they were teaching them to fear humans. It may have been the fledglings' first encounter with a human. The more mature of the two baby crows stayed put on the park bench in obvious conflict. His parents screamed of danger as I advanced, but he saw the nut I had for him. He was too inexperienced to make a wise choice, so he stayed, but, torn by the adult birds' alarm calls, he decided to caw weakly at me. I stifled my laughter. I didn't want to abuse the fragile trust the adults had for me or take advantage of their naïve youngster. I could easily have walked up and petted this bird, but instead I kept my distance and gently tossed the baby a nut. He took it without hesitation, and I left him and his family in peace.

It appeared that, much like human children, the young crows observed their parents' actions as well as their commands. "Do as we say, not as we do," I could imagine the elders admonishing after I left. Had the young crow been too inexperienced to understand the basic alarm call to flee danger, or had he been caught up in a more cerebral dilemma and weighing the choice before him? He had seen his parents behaving in an ambivalent way toward this human, first calling with alarm, then accepting the gift of food, and finally encouraging him to run from me. What was a young bird supposed to make of such a lesson? It was clear, to me at least, that this novice crow had been using his brainpower to make a choice rather than reacting blindly to his parents' demands. In some instances such behavior could get a bird killed, yet in this case the fledgling's observations had led to a positive outcome.

This encounter with the young Parkers provided the first concrete evidence that the area crows had been successful in their nesting attempts. By extrapolating backwards, I calculated that, at least for this family, hatching had taken place in the late weeks of May. That meant they had been incubating these two young crows during the last part of April. The location of the nest remained a mystery.

I discovered yet more proof of successful nesting a few days later, in the early morning hours. Pulled from my bed by strange crow calls, I slipped into shorts and a T-shirt and took off in the direction of the squalling. Like the honking of a goose mixed with a choking, insistent cry, the noises led me to the street behind the alley. There, I came upon the Scrap family, accompanied by two brand-new members of their tribe. Beaks wide and wings fluttering, the babies begged for whatever it was the adults were eating. As soon as I was sighted, the whole family screamed in fear, scrambling to get away from me as though they had never seen a human before, much less me. Once again surprised by their reaction, I concluded that they were trying to teach their babies to avoid evil humans and would refine the lesson later. I chased after them for a few moments before deciding I did not want to be humiliated any further by their rejection.

These were the first baby crows I had ever seen in my life. I felt grateful to have witnessed a sight some people take for granted, some are blind to, and some will never see. Each of the babies had a fresh look, their feathers barely used, and their shining minds starving to take in each new wonder.

8

Caws for Celebration

The time of year had come when all of nature crowded into the yard, making the empty spaces seem smaller and greener. The shrubs reached out to me, losing their spring shyness in bursts of new growth. There was much to be done in the garden. Weeds sprouted and threatened to start a gang war if they were not removed. As I pulled and pruned, trying to control the wildness of the world around me, I became aware of a presence watching me. Glancing around, I was pleased to see a crow in the small evergreen in front of Winona's tree watching the progress of my work. I wondered briefly if one of the Scraps had decided to begin using this lookout, but I'd never seen them in this particular spot before.

My gut feelings alerted me that this was an important occurrence, and I studied the crow, noting its elbows to confirm that it was not Fodderwing, my boldest and most likely suspect. This crow appeared winded, as if from a long flight; its beak was open in an apparent attempt to cool down. A crow that had not been flying long distances during the past few months, due to tending a nest, might be winded from a shorter flight. If her mate had been providing most of the nutrition for both her and the kids, she might have lost the stamina to fly easily to this part of her territory. Was it Winona? Had she returned for a visit, or had she finally been freed from the duties of the nest long enough to make this journey?

Hopeful, I searched my pockets for a nut to toss on the roof. Without hesitation, as though expecting the ritual, she descended to the roof, just a few feet above my head. "Where have you been?" I whispered as she took the food. Of course, she didn't answer, but even on her best day, Winona would never have answered such an inquiry. I was convinced that it was not a newly emboldened member of the Scrap family. I tried to determine exactly who it was. The same crow returned several times over the next few days, each time appearing winded. Once, the crow landed right above me on the telephone wire and did not even flinch as my sheltie barked her hello. The crow good-naturedly acknowledged the dog, as if having missed even the minor inconveniences of home. I came to realize it was indeed Winona by her slightly smaller head, her way of perching low on her elbows, and the way her left foot sometimes turned inward slightly. Even without the transient triangle shaped patch near her eye, I recognized her by her relationship to Wilbur.

The glorious return of the W's, like most things crow, was not as I had imagined. Expecting that whatever circumstances had led them away would release them all at once, freeing them to return to me as dramatically as they had left, I found the reality less spectacular. Instead, their integration back into my life was as slow as it was welcome.

At first, they appeared separately. Winona would visit the back garden, and Wilbur would meet me in the park after work. They were both more relaxed than I had seen them in a long while, and gone was any reticence to resume our old relationship. Wilbur had changed though—he looked ragged and was missing his tail feathers! Navigating like a ship without a rudder, he made his way through the air, beating his wings ever more fiercely to keep going. I worried about what could have happened to him and imagined a cat or a hawk snatching for and barely missing him—sparing his life, but not his tail. Perhaps it was something less heroic, like ectoparasites or an unusual molt.

Winona had also changed: she now acted downright friendly toward me. She began sitting for hours on the light post in front of my house, waiting for me to provide her with nuts. When I threw them down, she barely hesitated before snatching them up. She lingered at my feet to eat some of the nuts before flying with the excess to the railroad tracks. For a few days I believed this crow was Willy. I could identify Wilbur by his tail. I knew a baby would not be this tame toward me, and I found it hard to believe that Winona would act this way. Sometimes Wilbur would join this crow and sit for an hour or more on the light post just watching the traffic go by. It was becoming apparent that Willy was no longer with the family.

I wondered if Willy's absence had caused Winona to move up in rank, changing her role in the family and, consequently, her attitude toward me. Could I have interpreted as aloofness something else, like submissiveness? Did she feel more confident and dominant without Willy around?

I fretted over Willy, and that day in February came back to me in a flash. He had said good-bye to me because he had known then that he would not be returning home with his family. But what had happened to him?

As I reoriented myself to the W's return, I kept a sharp eye out for fledgling crows. Occasionally, unidentified crows appeared in or near the maple tree in the front yard. Thinking it was Winona or Wilbur, I would approach them, only to have them flee and scream at me. They did not look like babies, but I couldn't be sure. For a time I wondered if they were helpers at the W's nest, children from a previous year who had followed their parents back to the home territory for the day. As I watched them fly off, I noticed that their wings looked moth-eaten and used that characteristic to identify them. I still did not know if Wilbur and Winona had been successful parents. I had assumed that young crows, having wings and minds of their own, would follow their parents everywhere. But Wilbur and Winona were alone most of the time.

I was awakened one morning by the sound of baby crows being fed. Like bleating lambs they besieged their caretakers for food. "Baaaaa, baaaaa," they cried. Leaping out of bed and grabbing a microphone and a mini disc recorder, I followed the calls to the area behind the railroad tracks. Since I did not want to break the law or tear my clothing by scaling the six-foot wire fence to the railroad property, I stood listening in the weedy undergrowth across from my house. Wilbur acknowledged me as he flew overhead toward the source of his babies' cries. A gargled choking sound followed. Based on the extraordinary racket of feeding time, one might conclude that the fledglings are being killed.

Suddenly everything made sense to me. The babies had been there behind the fence all along, waiting quietly in the secluded safety behind the railroad tracks. Wilbur and Winona had spent hours on the light post in front of my house babysitting their charges, whom they had dropped off in an area where they could explore the world in relative isolation. In due time, I would witness their debut.

Even though the W's had come back to stay, their visits to the roof had been sporadic at best. Rather, they called me to meet them in the park, or waited for me in front of the house. The Scrap family was not going to give up control of the garage roof that easily, having gotten used to this convenience of their adopted territory. Many caw wars erupted over food. When I put the food out, no crows would land, preferring instead to call insults back and forth. Any crow that decided to descend on the food while the other side was present was risking attack, so they mostly tried to settle this territory dispute by "talking." If only I could have been privy to the meaning of their endless stream of caws.

One evening as the sun broke free from the summer storm clouds and a rainbow formed over the east, I tried to make my feelings known to the Scrap family, as if they could understand. A Scrap crow landed on the roof then flew to the wire above the yard, stretching his neck in an anxious way. I tossed nuts. Cawing exploded from every direction. Crows began flying everywhere, cawing madly, each side challenging the other to a duel. The action was quick and difficult to follow, but I spotted Wilbur (sans tail) circling low and deliberate right over my head. He then flew to the corner of the park, requesting—I was convinced—that I follow. Taking up a post underneath the perch of the cawing Winona, I stood in solidarity with my adopted crow family. I believed I was letting the Scraps know whose side I was on. I had to. I would have fed them all if they would have allowed it, but crows have their rules. I had to follow them in order to be accepted as an honorary member of the flock. I stood with Wilbur and Winona for a few minutes as they called to the Scraps. It was a turning point. The W's were back and they were reclaiming their old space. Whatever was said during this exchange seemed to settle the matter. From that point on, the Scraps began to fade from the picture, resuming their status as neighbors and ceasing to demand the rights to the roof. It seemed strange that my actions would have had any effect on the outcome of the battle, and it was more likely that something had ensued between the groups outside my range of observation. Perhaps other food sources were plentiful enough for the Scraps, and they did not care to expend their energy defending a handful of peanuts and some chicken bones.

9

Young Crows

Fighting the urge to stay in bed on Saturday morning and relishing my lack of obligation for the day, I made my way to the far end of the park—bleary eyed—to observe the Parkers and their newly fledged babies. It was too early in the morning for the baseball players, the fair-weather runners, and the mothers with children who played on the swings. The only creatures in the park were me, my dog, and the population of birds who had been awake since just before sunrise. As I shushed through the wet grass, my socks were already becoming wet and uncomfortable through my thin leather moccasins. I cursed my rush to get out the door in favor of taking the time to select adequate footwear.

I saw three crows ahead of me, halfway between the Parker and W territories. There are two light posts in this area, and the crows alighted on them to attract my attention. I thought it must have been Wilbur and Winona, because the Parkers had not yet learned this trick of begging from the posts. But technically, the W's were too far out of their range. The Parkers defended this area, and it would be brazen for the W's to cross here and risk the ill will of their neighbors. There were two adult crows and one baby. The adults took many nuts from me, and the baby begged for a share. Both of the adults barked at him, annoyed, raising the feathers on their heads as they did.

The crow family followed me to a tree, where I sat on the ground watching them. Their behavior was too tame for the Parker family, and I realized it was not they. All the crows had intact tails, so I concluded that it couldn't have been the W's, either. The largest crow strolled closer and closer to me, undaunted by my dog watching from the end of her leash. His baby followed at his heels, willing to unlearn his fear of humans without questioning his teacher. At an impressionable age, less than thirty days from the nest, this baby could have become attached to anyone who fed it. I was surprised that these crows trusted me within a few feet of their baby. He learned quickly from the adults how to act around me and that I was handing out free food. I tossed a nut his way, and he made a feeble attempt to open it after watching carefully how the adults were manipulating theirs. Unsuccessful, he gave up and asked once again to be fed. The larger of the two crows stuffed a piece of his cracked nut into the youngster's opened beak.

There was a glimmer of a light inside my head, and I stared in wonder at the large adult crow before me. He seemed to read my thoughts and stepped a few feet closer, answering my unspoken wish for a good look. A joy rushed to the center of my chest as my eyes began to tear over, and the realization dawning brought a moment I would carry with me for life. It was Willy. He'd come back with his young offspring. I understood now why he had left his parents. And so much of the past made sense.

It was clear he had established his own territory, next to his parents'. He had abandoned his old life for this, a family of his own. I had been sure I would never see him again, but here he stood before me, as if to say, "Don't you recognize me?"

But who was the adult crow tagging along with him—his new wife, or could it have been Grandma Winona, visiting with her son and checking out his progress as a first-time father? In days to come I was able to establish with reasonable certainty that it was in fact Winona, as Willy's wife was less than enamored with me and didn't quite understand the whole human-crow bond.

Some research indicates that males ready to breed inherit a share of the natal territory or don't move very far from home when they do set up housekeeping. The Parkers had loosely defended that portion of the park, so I was wondering now if Wilbur and Willy's mysterious actions earlier in the year had been visits to the Parker family to court one of its single females. Could Willy have married the girl next door? Or perhaps, turning my assumptions on their ears, Willy was a female and had selected for her mate a Parker male who now occupied a fragment of his natal territory. It was interesting that Wilbur would have accompanied his offspring on what I now believed were Willy's attempts to form a partnership with one of the Parkers. Perhaps his father's status as a breeding male from next door had helped Willy break into the Parker clan. I recalled how relatively quickly the Parkers had accepted me as friend and, in particular, the boldness of one of their members. I had noticed the way this crow had tucked his head and run toward me, and the thought crossed my mind now that it could have been Willy. At the time, I had chalked my impressions up to missing Willy. But now I was sure of his identity, and I became even surer as he and his new family continued to visit over the summer.

Willy's remarkable return was a highlight of my summer, and the joy it brought me was surpassed only by the fact that he had brought three little ones with him. Proudly leading them toward me, he taught them of our friendship. They were quick to learn and eager to trust me. I sat on the ground as all four gathered around me, waiting for me to toss a nut and anxious for their turns. The circle closed as they slowly came closer to me, and at times when one crow had my attention, another of the young ones crept remarkably near, just outside my field of vision. When I turned my head, I was startled by its presence there. The fledglings were irresistibly cute. Their eyes were just turning from the blue of the nest to a more adult brown. Their inquisitive nature colored their view of the world. One in particular had become my early favorite, mainly because I could always recognize his crooked tail, but also because he was much less afraid of me than the others.

He appeared to be an especially gentle soul, quite the opposite of the stereo-typical crow. At times I wondered if he could have been "different" in some ways—a nerdy crow the other members of Corvus family might shun. The fact that he was not an aggressive, brash Corvid seemed to garner him less respect among his family members but only endeared him to me more. He was like a simple child: he seemed to understand the sunshine but not the ways of defend-ing the territory. He picked at dandelions and at his toes, and he seemed to be trying to make sense of the world while the others were off slaying bugs to eat—and enjoying the process. The crow with the crooked tail appeared to prefer studying the bugs and noticing their pretty colors.

Perhaps, whatever it was that made him a strange crow also made him less fearful of me. He crept ever closer, causing the other crows watching from their perches to call out in alarm. But he only looked up at them, as if to say, "She would never hurt me."

In fact, I had already met this crow before I knew he was Willy's offspring. I had been meandering toward the far end of the park one day, when a crow perched on the fence near the maintenance garage caught my eye. I had assumed he was one of the Parker youngsters and had approached him slowly, thinking he would fly off before I got too near. To my amazement, he held still and, with no other birds around to tell him what he should do, let me walk right up to him. I did not press my advantage, but I did toss him a nut to reward him for his calmness. I was quite surprised when he descended without hesitation to pick at it. This tameness is not a useful attribute in a wild crow, but it served my needs quite well!

He was a scrawny little fellow, and I had noticed his bent tail right away. It could have been his first day out of the nest for all I knew. I looked around for any sign of his parents, but when I didn't see anyone, I assumed he had wandered off on his own and that they had no idea he was getting himself into this type of trouble. Thinking back now, I wondered if Willy had witnessed the whole encounter and remained silent because he saw no harm in his offspring getting to know me. I would never forget the way this fledgling with the bent tail had looked perched up near the trash cans, wondering what to do next in such a big new place.

I didn't know why his tail canted off at such an odd angle, but it helped me find his name. He became CT (Crooked Tail) Parker from that day forward. Genetics, a tumor, or a spinal deformity could have caused his tail abnormality. He looked like a weak crow, and I wondered if he would even survive very long. I love rooting for the underdog, and I had said good-bye to CT that first day hoping we would meet again.

CT Parker had the same gentle nature exhibited by both his father, Willy, and his grandfather, Wilbur. For this reason I thought of CT as male. I never dwelled much on the gender of the crows, however, since there was almost no possibility that I could ever prove the validity of such intuitive guesses.

As the summer progressed, I met with Willy and his family on a regular basis. He occupied a rigidly defined area of the park, and even his original family chased him if he got too close to the border. It was both interesting and enlightening that he was no longer welcome in his old home territory, and except for the one visit from Winona, the W family never showed any indication that they ever had known him. Willy's mate remained distant and wild, although she consented to taking nuts from me. Something prevented her from unlearning her distrust of humans, for even though she had witnessed Willy's devoted trust in me, she remained aloof. Sometimes when Willy was away and she had brought the three young ones to the park alone, she would become nervous at their clamoring near me as though I were the ice cream man. They ignored her warning calls, as if to say, "Dad said it was OK."

I was beguiled by the antics of the young crows and never tired of watching as they clambered around wolfing down nuts almost faster than I could toss them. With all the extra beaks to feed, my bulging pockets would empty quickly, making me wish I had brought even more. One day, as Willy finished the last of my stock, he looked up at me asking for another. Desperate to keep him a little longer, I began whispering to him. I told him how much I missed his visits to the house and how I wished he could come for some pizza, just like the old days. I told him how I had feared I would never see him again, how I had worried, and how much I loved him. He studied me intently with his dark eye, standing stock-still. Then he flashed his nictitating membrane, and I felt the electricity of emotion pass between us.

I know from experience that birds are emotional creatures, extremely sensitive to humans' state of mind. Having kept pet birds for over fifteen years, I was familiar with their ways of communicating and receiving feelings. I found crows similar to parrots in their ability to read human intent. Whereas dogs seem to read body language, birds seem able somehow to look into the human heart and see what is written on its secret pages.

I was surprised by how long Willy stood still, listening to me and absorbing my feelings. Suddenly he flew to a branch nearby and began serenading me with a crow song the likes of which I had never heard. It was a song filled with rattles, melodious warbling, coos, and a lilting woo woo. I was astonished by his display. It seemed to me that Willy was singing of happiness and love. His heart was full, he was saying. His song seemed a description of his adventures and travels during the time we had been apart. He seemed to sing from the very depths of his being, and I was filled with the awe of having crossed the bridge into the world of another species.

Watching how the adult crows treated their offspring gave me new insights into the nature of crows, not to mention a completely new set of personalities to interact with. The W babies were beginning to show themselves in public. I saw Winona feeding them on the building roofs near the railroad tracks. I counted two new lives. One came with Wilbur to beg from the streetlight in front of the house and then followed him to the railroad tracks, where I heard him begging for his share of the nuts. Crows-in-training, the young W's mimicked their parents' actions in order to learn the ropes.

It was a slow process to get the W fledglings to trust me as much as their parents did. They seemed older than the Parker babies I had met at the park and thus had developed a stronger fear instinct. The W's had kept them hidden from me during their most vulnerable period, when I probably could have picked them up and petted them if I had chosen to. Crow parents protect their precious young with everything they have. I knew these young W's would eventually model their behavior toward me after their parents' behavior, so I was not worried. It seemed Wilbur and Winona had determined the right time to begin introducing them to their human friend.

In early July, I took a vacation from work and spent time watching crows. One lazy afternoon, the entire W family came for a nap in Winona's tree. I used the opportunity to sit quietly with them, so the babies could become used to my presence and the fact that I stared at them through binoculars. I counted three babies—a surprise, as I had been sure there were only two. But this third young bird disappeared soon after that day, never to be seen again. Was it one of the moth-eaten crows I had seen earlier, a helper at the nest? Or had some tragedy occurred, causing the loss of one of the young? Would a youngster from another family tag along to play with the W children for the afternoon? Did he belong to Willy's clan?

The wee W's were becoming noisier and more demanding. I thought their parents might have been weaning them, which meant forcing them to find food for themselves more often. It seemed to frustrate the babies, and they called for food more often. All this crying seemed to try Winona's patience, and I saw her rebuff a fledgling's attempt to even sit next to her. As if she felt her work was done, she had shifted the responsibility for the little ones to Wilbur's Crow Finishing School. The fledglings tagged along with him quite often, while Winona was off somewhere else. He was a patient father, sometimes entertaining them with small toys, such as a dried up old rib bone. He dangled it in front of one of his charges until the young crow grabbed it and began to manipulate it with a curious beak. A bone from one of our long ago shared meals now had become a plaything for young crows.

Oddly-shaped shiny objects began to appear in my yard, and I wondered if it was possible that they were crow toys carried from the nest area and dropped there. A crow's penchant for shiny objects is sometimes called a persistent myth. The appearance of these small items coincided with the movement of the young crows in my area. They were mostly rivets from the tops of buildings or silver pieces of the material used to fashion heating ducts. Perhaps the crows had been visiting a construction site. It was hard to imagine how these pieces would have found their way into my yard if not dropped there on the wing.

The Scrap family's reluctant surrender of the feeding roof had allowed the W's to spend more time in their old spots. I was beginning to get a closer look at the young crows. Of the two W offspring, one was obviously older and more developed in his abilities. If he had been the first in the clutch to hatch, he could have been up to several weeks older than his sibling. Eggs from the same period destroyed by circumstance or predation might also have been replaced, which could also account for the age difference. Either way, this difference was fortuitous for me, because with four crows around, it was getting hard to tell who was who. The older fledgling reminded me of Winona. He came to the yard for visits, sitting on the wire overhead for long periods just watching me. I had extended periods, therefore, to study his face. To my eye, it was unique. In fact, it reminded me of an eagle's. The feathers that extended down the top of his beak were prominent, adding to this illusion. He had the fresh, shiny appearance of a young bird. I would have named him Eagle, but his name had to begin with a W, in keeping with his heritage. Instead I called him Weagle. I pronounced it *weejel*.

Weagle was just learning to gather and crack his own nuts. He had studied his elders carefully and had spent a part of every day working up the courage to land on the garage roof to get a nut of his own. Without interference from the Scrap family, it was simply Weagle against his own nerves. It struck me that it must have been difficult for an inexperienced bird to judge the distance to the roof and maneuver a landing onto this foreign surface. Although more advanced than his clumsy nest mate, Weagle had still to learn the finer points of flight and control of his machinery.

Wilbur had developed a new habit of landing on my neighbor's roof, in a spot where he could see me sitting in my chair, and visiting with me from there. Sometimes we bowed to each other. He would bow, and I would imitate his exaggerated neck bend. It was unclear to me whether he could recognize my feeble attempt for the gesture it was. After a time I realized he was spending his time on the neighboring roof not so much to visit with me as to show his charges that I was acceptable company. He sat calmly for long periods, until one of the fledglings joined him there. Perhaps he had altered his perch to make it easier for them to spot him or to provide a landing surface more stable than a swaying telephone line. Once one of the little ones had joined him, he sat quietly in a reassuring manner before flying to the garage roof and picking up a nut—illustrating not only how the routine goes but also that I am a safe human.

The younger of the two birds had a strong personality. He was easy to recognize, because he was so much smaller than the rest of the crows. His feathers were missing in some spots, giving him a scruffy look. He had the pronounced brownish cast of a young bird. Despite his size and scraggly appearance, he soon became top crow! The whole family deferred to him, letting him eat first and generally letting him get away with murder. He stole their food, pecked at them, and had the manners of a hurricane. He threw tantrums regularly: screaming and protesting if he didn't get the piece of food he wanted. The sound of his caw was immature, and mammalian. Like a kitten with a scruffy voice, he whined and moaned about much of what happened to him.

There were days when, despite his strong spirit, I wondered if this younger crow had a chance in the world. He was extremely uncoordinated and seemed to take weeks to learn how to eat on his own. The simple act of opening his beak and taking in food seemed to elude him. He stabbed and pecked at it without getting much of anything into his belly. He looked weak, sometimes showing up with a slight limp. For these reasons I decided to call him Waif.

Weagle, the opportunist, took advantage of his younger sibling many times. Poor Waif would spend up to five minutes cracking a peanut, only to inexplicably allow the nutmeat to roll down into the gutter. Swiftly, the more experienced Weagle would snap it up—even before Waif had figured out that anything had gone wrong. Although the whole family stepped aside to let Waif have his share of food first, he often made poor choices. Once he grabbed a carrot out of a pile of chicken stew, probably because it was a bright orange color. I could almost hear Weagle laughing, because crows *hate* vegetables. I have seen many a crow painstakingly pick minute particles of vegetable off a leftover Subway sandwich before eating it.

Waif was also a food waster, much to the irritation of his mother. Fish was a big favorite with the crows, and it was not unusual to have all four begging from my plate like spoiled dogs. They could even tell when I was bringing home food by the takeout bags I carried, and they would gather around before I could even take the food from the bags. One day, after sharing my fish with the crows, I sat back to watch them. Waif was wrestling with a big crunchy piece in the evergreen over the roof. I felt as though I could read Winona's mind as she swooped down and grabbed the piece away from him, because I was thinking the same thing: Waif would make a mess of that valuable piece of fish. He would drop most of it on the ground to be stolen by squirrels. Winona had taken it from him to store for a later time. He screamed loudly in protest, "Not fair, not fair!" But he went along with Winona's decision, probably because he had already eaten his share and was not so much hungry as just being little Waif.

Waif still begged for food from his parents or made a begging call before eating food he had found himself. Once in a great while Wilbur would quickly shove pieces of food down Waif's throat, with an almost furtive, "Don't tell your mother" air. It was hard to resist Waif's helplessness, and sometimes, against my better judgment, I cracked Waif's nuts for him. And then I broke them in half so they wouldn't roll down the roof and get away. For all his clumsy foolishness, Waif seemed to wield some unspoken power over the rest of his family. Did he have a bad temper, causing the others to fear him? Or did they defer to him because they sensed his weakness? He was an odd mix of power and fragility. One thing was certain; it was hard not to love him.

The youngest W's were beginning to accept me, especially Waif, who had met me at a stage when he was more likely to accept a human friend. He stood much closer to me on the roof than the others as I threw his food, showing very little fear of my presence. Once he had mastered the art of cracking a nut, he stayed on the roof eating one after another. He tossed the empty shells in my direction, as if to say, "Done, I need another." Sometimes if I was looking down reading, he would make a small barking sound to alert me that he was ready for more. But the biggest thrill of all came as I was driving up the alley, coming home from work. I could see all four crows waiting for me in Winona's tree, and, with the windows rolled down, I could hear the squall of Waif's begging heralding my arrival. He had cast me in the role of surrogate adult crow and expected food when he saw me.

Baby crows spend a lot of time practicing vocalizations, and they produce some odd sounds as they experiment with their new voices. Early on, Waif began imitating what sounded to me like my dog barking. It was a mixture of caws and barks that, despite his valiant attempts, still ended up sounding like a crow's call. Perhaps he chose the song of a dog because he felt it would help him sound like the fierce warrior he might someday become. My most creative vocalist, Waif, could always be counted on for an early morning serenade. His voice was recognizable from a distance due to the sheer variety of his mutterings. Once, when to my ear he seemed just outside my bedroom window, I got up to find him parked on the garage roof, singing while waiting for his breakfast.

Waif and Weagle made a habit of stopping by my house first thing in the morning and perching on the garage roof, waiting for me to get up. Baby crows are very honest, just like human children. Gone was Winona's nonchalant attitude that said, "Just happened to be passing by, and anyway, I always sit on this wire." The babies' motives were transparent, and they didn't care if I knew it.

Weagle seemed to appoint himself town crier and always called to his parents (or Waif, if he were tardy that day) when I put out the chow. One day when I gave them something Weagle particularly liked, he "forgot" to call the others and instead immediately began eating. When the rest of the clan descended, he quickly cawed to them with his beak full, as if to say, "Oh I was just about to call you."

Weagle also took on the role of older sibling when sharing the finer points of caching with the witless Waif. I watched once as Weagle purposefully dropped a noodle for Waif and then showed him how to hide the extra pieces underneath the metal roof cap. The lesson was lost on Waif. He watched Weagle carefully cache the food, then he immediately uncached and ate it. Weagle patiently tolerated the impish behavior of his younger nestmate.

The two spent many hours calling to each other, exchanging odd vocalizations from neighboring trees. This calling back and forth could go on for thirty minutes at a time. I enjoyed hearing it and stopped what I was doing to listen. It apparently could get on an adult crow's nerves, however, because other crows seemed to plead with the youngsters to stop it already. Perhaps they were annoyed by the nonsense babble of the young, but nonsense or not, these verbal exchanges appeared to be the foundation of the bond between the fledgling crows.

10

Seasonal Fluctuations in Crow Society

It was a summer of plenty, as crows were everywhere and my friendships with them bountiful. I spent almost every free moment observing them, whether following the Parkers around the park or puzzling over the actions of my home groups. One lazy afternoon, I was sitting in my yard on the bench near the pond. I could see the W's in the maple tree before me, and I wondered if they would come to the garage roof when I was sitting just below it and thus was out of their field of vision. As an experiment I threw some nuts for them and sat down again on the bench. In the glass on the back door, I could see the top of the roof behind me Wilbur did come to the roof, but he sat on the peak for a few moments. I wondered why he hadn't taken the nuts, but when I got up to look, I found that the blue jays had made off with them, leaving none for Wilbur. I guessed that Wilbur had been waiting for me to notice him there. What method did he believe I could employ? Did he think I had a special ability to know where he was because I had appeared to know in the past? Or was he also using the reflection in the glass and inferring that I could see him as he could see me? He did eventually come for the nuts as I sat there, as did the rest of his family, proving at least that they trusted me enough to get close without keeping me in their line of sight.

Later that week, Wilbur and Winona were sitting on the light post in front of the house. I offered them peanuts, but they didn't seem hungry. Both were sitting with their beaks open. It was not a hot day, and I couldn't imagine that they were trying to cool off. I had been watching them awhile, when all at once they begin regurgitating something onto the street below. Crows often produce pellets of indigestible material much like owls. Anxious to see what such pellets might consist of, I hurried over for a closer look. It appeared to be the seeds from a type of large berry. I was excited by my find and collected the seeds, hoping to locate other crow hangouts by identifying the berry. The location of the W's other stop-

65

ping points and the extent of their territory had been an ongoing source of mystery to me. I had speculated that they flew to the golf course and the forest preserve by tracing the direction of their flight on a map. Since flying along behind them was out of the question, I hoped the berries would provide a clue as to where the W's wanderings took them.

Wherever the family went when they left my area it could not have been very far. I had noted the time they arrived in the morning, not long after first light. Similarly, they left in the evening for their resting spot only a few minutes before dark Perhaps their territory wasn't one continuous circle, I theorized, but was more a hopscotch of patches between my house and the golf course. They might defend these favorite patches—the most interesting and fruitful spots—from other crows but not claim the whole expanse as their own.

Over the summer months, I became very attached to the Parkers. Since I didn't see them every day, as I did the W's, they were always grateful for my treats and crowded around for their turns. The majority of the time as I approached, if Willy was in the area he would fly straight for me, either circling overhead and turning to look at me or landing in the distance and walking toward me as I walked toward him. I always knew it was he, and I called him by name. I thought by that point he probably recognized that his name was Willy, just as a dog knows its name. Eventually the rest of the Parkers adjusted their schedules to mine and began waiting for me at the appointed times on the fence near the baseball diamond. This routine caused consternation for the W's. For even though the Parkers were keeping within their boundary, the W's did not want them taking food from me—period! It caused tremendous conflict between the groups, and the W's flew at the Parkers in an agitated manner. Calling excitedly, they worked at driving this interloping family away.

I felt horrible hurting the W's feelings in this way. I did not want to insult the W's or cause them any distress. I always fed them first, but this concession was not enough for them. The first few times the W's reacted this way, I felt I could get away with it, pretending to be a dumb human who did not understand crow customs. I found it odd that Wilbur and Winona would deprive their own son of his share of food. After all, they knew I was Willy's friend also. Perhaps once a crow left the immediate circle, he was automatically treated as an outsider when it came to defending territory. In what instances might Willy be welcome in his old circle? When mobbing a threat for certain—but would there be other times? These conflicts in the park caused me once again to wonder about what familial ties might bind the W's and the Scraps.

The W's went so far as to insist that the Parkers not even sit on the fence by the baseball diamond when I was around, even if I wasn't close enough to feed them. It was as if they understood that the other group was showing itself because they knew it would draw me to them. "She belongs to us!" the W's seemed to caw.

During these skirmishes I noticed that crows draw circles in the air by flying around things, as though drawing an imaginary line around what is theirs. I saw them do this to show other crows where they feel their territory begins and ends. A few times, they circled over my head, as though to claim me as their own or, in the W's case, to tell me to follow them back into W territory, as though being merely human, I couldn't comprehend that I had crossed a boundary line. I hoped they thought I was dumb and not insensitive to their feelings.

I made an effort to meet up with the Parker clan when I knew the W's were elsewhere. The rest of the time, I just felt guilty about the situation and hoped I was not causing damage to my bond with the W's. It was hard to know if they trusted me less because I had gone against their wishes.

During that summer, I spent several days vacationing away from home. I wondered how my crows would react to my absence. Having spent the past year feeding them every day, predictable as a clock, I wondered if they would miss me. I tried to give them extra rations as I packed up the car. I felt helpless to explain what was happening as they watched me get ready to leave. I was taking my dog, too.

Although I knew they were perfectly capable of fending for themselves, I thought about them often while I was gone. When I arrived home, I saw no crows in the area. I began unpacking the car. My dog was "helping" by barking at flies and other dangerous things. I hoped my crows would hear her and know I was back. Not long after, I heard a Scrap crow give a one-note caw similar to the one I had heard during the winter heralding my arrival home from work. And it came from the same spot, too. I thought this was merely coincidence, but soon a baby W flew over my head making its juvenile caw, followed by Winona, who landed on the light post in front of my house to beg for nuts. After I had given her a nut, she seemed to show no change in behavior toward me, and I accepted the fact that the crows had gone about their lives in my absence. Then a most unusual thing happened.

Suddenly, like pennies from heaven, crows appeared from every direction. There were Scraps, Parkers and W's all intermingling to circle over my head and caw. Between ten and twelve crows swooped low and then rose into the sky, calling a song I had never heard before. Their voices had a sweet lilt, and their calls ended on a bouncing note. They hovered above me at times, and I was lost in the surreal moment. They appeared to dance in the sky with joy. I stood watching them, riding the waves of my feelings. Were they celebrating my return? Could they have thought I had been injured or killed? Had I reappeared after they had given up hope?

When it was over, I headed back to my yard still incredulous over the display. Had I imagined it? Had it been the wishful thoughts of a raving lunatic? But my niece's face told me it had been real, as the words tumbled from her, "Did you see what the crows did! Did you see how happy they were to see you?" She had been watching from a distance, sharing this amazing experience. It was then that I knew I had not imagined this sky dance or its significance.

Despite the emotional nature of my homecoming, I made several observations that bear mentioning. After this event I came to believe that the W's and the Scraps had an alliance that superseded any squabble they may have had over territory or who gets the food on the roof. Their display showed them joining to welcome back a friend who had gone missing. Much like the allegiance they might share in mobbing an owl, this happy event brought the warring factions together. Perhaps they had even communicated with each other in my absence, fearing that I had vanished. Perhaps the W's had envisioned my beheading by a hawk, as I had when they had disappeared to make their nest.

Additionally, since the W's had limited my summer contact with the Scraps and the Parkers, how had they known I was missing in order to celebrate my return? I didn't think the Scraps had been constantly watching my house and yard from a distance, so it occurred to me that the W's might have had a way to convey to them that I was gone. "Have you seen the girl?" Wilbur might have inquired. This kind of communication between groups could have a useful social function: to alert the larger group when one of the flock was missing. My experiences with crows had left no doubt that they cared about one another, and concern for a missing member would be a natural extension of that caring.

I constantly marveled at these wonderful birds, and I couldn't understand how people could pass them by without noticing them or realizing what special creatures they were. After my welcome home, I felt I had succeeded in reaching a level of understanding with wild creatures that only few people know is possible. The crows' intelligence and willingness to allow me into their circle touched places in me left barren by generations of disconnect between humans and the natural world.

It had always been a dream of mine to convince the crows to land in my tiny back garden, but they never seemed amenable to this idea. Even last winter when the snows made it impossible for them to cross the garage roof on their short legs, my asking them to take food from the ground just beyond my gate had been greeted with suspicion and trepidation. As the days grew shorter and fall shook loose with its soggy orange, red, and gold, however, I made another attempt at inviting the W family to land in the garden. I had known the two W youngsters for several months by that time, and I decided to capitalize on the new genera-tion's bolder acceptance of me.

One day in late October, after the crows had had their breakfast, they came back several times, calling to me from their perches in the garden and interrupt-ing my coffee time by begging for more food. After several rounds, I decided they were being unusually greedy and that they had collected enough for their needs. I wondered if they sensed bad weather coming and were stockpiling supplies. I decided to use this opportunity to test the waters. Since I knew I wouldn't be depriving them of a necessary meal, I opened the back door, checked to make sure they were watching me, then threw a pile of nuts onto the ground in the middle of the garden. I was sure they wouldn't come down for them, as they had never dared land in the yard before.

Weagle eyed the nuts skeptically and then to my surprise came to the edge of the roof. He tilted his head and used one eye to peer at them even more closely. He appeared to be considering coming down and landing in my garden! I held my breath and stepped back from the window so as not to jinx the moment or scare him away. But he decided against it and flew away. Drat! I knew he wouldn't come down. With all he had hauled away earlier that morning, he prob-ably would not have been motivated to dare a new trick. I stood by the window watching to see if he would return.

A few moments later, Weagle did come back, perching over the yard on the wire to check on the nuts. It seemed he had thought things over and come up with a plan. First, he flew to my neighbor's fence, which brought him closer to my yard than any crow had ever dared come before. The sight of him sitting qui-etly on the fence mesmerized me. He spent a few moments making sure the area was safe. Then, without warning, he swooped directly to the center of the yard and began gathering the nuts. Casting off any doubts he had had about the dan-gers of the yard, he sauntered around picking up the nuts and stacking them as his family looked on. Once Weagle had broken the ice, these visits to my yard became a regular occurrence. Waif copied his sibling without reservation, and even Wilbur tried it out once or twice, although he seemed more wary than his offspring.

I had never seen crows land in any of the tight yards in my neighborhood, and it probably had something to do with feeling safer in open spaces, where a crow is less likely to be surprised by an ambush from a hiding predator. Not knowing any better, Waif and Weagle soon became quite comfortable about visiting my garden. One morning, I peered out to find Waif calling to me from my garden bench. But an early cold snap dumped heaps and heaps of snow on the garden, ending for the time being the crow's visits to the ground. I hoped they wouldn't forget this new skill and waited patiently for the thaw.

In early November, just before the snows came, I was awakened by the sounds of crows on the railroad tracks. It was an unusual sounding disturbance: one crow was cawing as though its heart were breaking, in a tone that was both hurt and bewildered. The other crows sounded as though they were chasing something off. Having heard crows attacking a predator before, I had a reference for comparison, and the fear was missing in their voices. No, this sounded as though one of the young crows was being chased off the territory. There was an outburst of hysteria, an argument, but I had no sense there was an eminent danger. Then all was quiet. I had the feeling that whatever had happened had been both important and sad.

Only three crows came for breakfast that morning—Wilbur, Winona, and Weagle. My little Waif was missing. In the fall of each year many young crows gather in large flocks; perhaps Waif had been shooed off to seek his fame and fortune in one of these roaming groups. The W's territory may have been only large enough to support three crows. If Waif were a male crow, he would be more likely to leave the family early. According to crow researcher Carolee Caffrey, it is the female of the species that stays at home to serve as a helper at the nest. I thought I saw Waif a few weeks later in his usual spot on the telephone line—at least I hoped it was Waif. Perhaps he made this brief visit to let me know he was OK. He probably felt I could easily recognize him at a distance the same way he could easily recognize me. I missed that small and feisty crow marching back and forth across my garage roof, looking cross that I wasn't cracking nuts and tossing them to him. I looked for him always.

Although the Scraps were usually somewhere in the vicinity, something changed in early January that year, and they acted as though they should be allowed access to the garage roof once again. I saw that Fodderwing was still well, still sounding his hoarse, unusual call. Spook showed himself on his favorite distant perch from time to time. They started waiting for me in the morning, just as they had the year before, clearly remembering my schedule. But the W's were not leaving the territory, and each morning brought a standoff between the two groups.

Who would be the first to descend, touching off the inevitable melee? It was still too early to be thinking about nesting, although crows have been know to start this activity in February. The Scraps, however, like Christmas merchandise in October, seemed to be rushing the season. Perhaps food was scarce, and they had come back to take advantage. Each group seemed to know quite easily when the opposing side was not in the area, and they swooped down without hesitation to feed in a relaxed manner from the roof. It was a different scenario when both groups were present together, however. Neither side would relinquish control of the food. Caw wars once again become the order of the day.

It became more difficult to tell the crows apart, as the Scraps had become less furtive, making it harder to tell they are not the W's. I had to pay careful attention to the territory to which each of the birds returned.

I would be watching closely in the coming months as nesting began. There were new factors to consider. Weagle was still with the family and too young to breed, unlike Willy who had left last year to start his own nest. Would Weagle stay behind to guard the area and thus assure that the Scraps could not get a foothold? Would the W's attitude toward me remain static, and, furthermore, would the events of the past summer have proven to them that I was not a threat to their young? Perhaps they would even consider bringing their nest closer to my house.

In February, there were changes in the way the crows handled my park visits. No longer fighting the fact that I fed them all, they seemed to have negotiated some acceptance of each other. Somehow, all three families had worked out a peaceful arrangement. When I arrived, it was cause for celebration. Each family knew me in its own way and seemed to accept the fact that they must share me. Usually it was one of the Parkers who first spied me and called out to the others. This all points bulletin brought crows from every direction and every territory. It was a new twist to have the Scraps meet me in the park, but they crowded around, too, respecting the invisible lines that demarcated their borders. Although I felt emotionally closest to the W's, the Parkers came physically closest to me.

CT Parker was almost fearless, and we shared a special bond that allowed him to close the gap between us. There were times when I was sitting on the ground with the families looking on as CT crept to within three feet of me. The bystanders called out in alarm, but CT ignored them. I overheard the conversation of some humans as they passed. "They must know her," one remarked. Once, I took the chance of holding out a nut to CT. He turned his back on me quickly, but I was not insulted, because I felt the day might come when he could change his mind.

I tossed nuts, trying to be fair in my distribution, as my impatient Sheltie strained to continue her walk. "These pesky crows are a nuisance," she must have thought. I spun around in response to a call from a crow needing a nut. They cawed to get my attention, and at least in the park this seemed to have kept them from squabbling amongst themselves. I loved them all for different reasons, and I thought they had finally figured that out.

A late winter thaw freed the yard of snow, and the weather was reasonable enough to see if the crows remembered how to visit the garden. I shouldn't have worried. Not only was Weagle happy to stroll around, but several of the Scraps visited as well. Weagle showed no hesitation in coming down to the ground to collect nuts from the middle of the yard. He spent quite a bit of time there, drinking water out of the pond, hopping onto the bench, walking on the deck, and caching a few nuts—one under a large clump of dried ornamental grass and the other near a rock by the pond. I hoped my neighbor would not see the rather large slice of pizza Weagle stuffed in his rain gutter. I would have to remember to assure him that the crows would remember their hiding places and come back for the food they had cached. Luckily, he had become a crow fan himself and didn't mind their visits. He had even kept me apprised of their activities while I was away. "Wilbur came looking for you today," he reported one day, "and I told him, 'Come back later, she's not home yet.'"

Later that same week, I was surprised to find that not only one but two Scraps came down into the tiny garden to hunt for nuts and explore this new territory. Their activity did not go unnoticed by the W's, who flew at them, screaming and complaining. "Must we share everything with you?" they seemed to caw.

I had discovered what I thought was a new, separate family living adjacent to the Parkers. I'd named them the Courts, because they had come over to meet me near the tennis courts where my dog is allowed to run. I first met them one day after feeding my other families, when I noticed three crows sitting in the tree right next to the court. They watched my dog and me closely.

I could see they hadn't come with the Parkers, but I suspected they had been watching the feeding activities from a distance and had grown curious enough to approach. I tossed a few nuts in their direction, and they seemed interested. When they didn't come down right away, it was confirmation in my mind that they were "new" crows who didn't know me very well. One of the three eventually swooped low over the nuts and landed on another tree branch. But they waited until I left the area to finally collect them.

The next time I came back, sure enough, they were waiting in their courtside tree. I usually closed up all the doors of the tennis court, so my dog could run free, and I didn't have to worry about her safety. She spent her time herding her big metal sheep (cars) by running alongside the fence, barking and pushing them along. The Courts seem to find this activity very interesting. That day they even trusted me enough to come down and get their nuts while I was still standing nearby. I thought the Court family had accepted me so rapidly by relying on the judgment of their neighbors the Parkers and the Scraps. I guessed I was developing quite a reputation within the crow community.

The Courts must have realize that dogs can't run through fences and thus felt safe enough to land near us. My dog, however, thought the crows needed some rousting and despite constant admonitions from me began a game of chasing them. She especially liked dashing at them as they landed on the top of the fence to peer down at her.

The Scraps were also present, but they kept to the other side of the court in their own territory. My dog chased them, too, but since they knew her from home, they tolerated her antics in a good-natured way. I chased after her a little myself, to teach the crows about my relationship with her and show that she was indeed a friend. One of the Courts seemed to perceive this behavior immediately as play. This crow purposefully flew down to attract her attention and then allowed her to chase him. As this was not unlike a game two crows might play in the sky, it was not a stretch for him to correctly infer my playful intent. Some animals test a predator's abilities in order to hone their knowledge of the creature. The crow may have engaged with my dog for this purpose, but I believe he did it for fun. We all seemed to be having a good time together.

When March came in like a lion, the winds brought with them a surprise visitor. I was attracted by an odd crow sound, a sort of "Aaack, aaack," coming from three crows engaged in an odd dance across the street on the railroad tracks. Two crows are walking along one of the metal rails toward a third crow, who is responsible for this sound and who is sidestepping away from them. I wondered if it could be Wilbur and Winona chasing Weagle away. They did not seem aggressive toward the third crow, but they were obviously pushing him away. Were they trying to prevent him from taking food from their cache stations? I watched awhile then got some nuts and corn chips for them.

When I set out the food underneath the streetlight, four crows appeared. Who was this bird being pushed away on the tracks? Waif? I strained for any clues to its identity, but I could not identify it with any certainty. This crow knew all the ins and outs of the W's territory—where the food was cached, where to fly to eat—and he was also allowed to share the bounty I provided with the other three.

If this was Waif, why had he returned? Was he simply visiting, or had he fallen on hard times and come home for a meal and some blanket of familiarity? Was he following a drive to return to the family in time to help with that year's nest? Was he here to stay? Rejoicing at the possibility of Waif's return, I thought about how I would gladly crack every nut for him, just like the old days. At the very least, I was pleased to see he still existed.

A few days later, the weather changed again, and it became rainy and mild, perfect weather for crows foraging in the park. From my kitchen window, I saw four black dots amiably rummaging around near the mud puddle that formed like a small lake when it rained. Could it be Waif with the other W's again? Who else would be allowed to forage peacefully shoulder-to-shoulder with the other three? And who else would recognize me as a friend?

Reaching into my coat pocket, I found a nut waiting. I could always count on finding them in the pockets of my pants, shirts, and jackets. My dog scanned my clothing if I left it lying around, as she had discovered the secret to unleashing the unorthodox treats. I tossed a few nuts to the roof and waited to see who would come by. Only two of the four opted for the easy meal, and I identified them as Wilbur and Weagle. Later, after the nuts were gone, and I had returned to my business indoors, I saw a rather small crow marching back and forth on the garage roof. Waif was the only one who had ever marched around the roof when there was no food, as though he expected me to read his thoughts. He acted as though I *owed* the nuts to him and had been derelict in my duty. I opened the back door, and he waited on the roof as I tossed several nuts into the yard. He had lost a bit of tameness since I had last seen him, so I watched from behind the closed door through my binoculars. I notice the small white molt spot I had used to identify him the other day. He took the nuts and retreated to the park. It seems both Weagle and Waif have lost their red mouth lining. Even with one less marker I can use to identify them, this crow left no doubt as to his identity. He has left an indelible impression with his strong persona and won my heart forever.

Wilbur and his missing tail

Weagle (L) Waif (R) on feeding roof

Crow Meeting hosted by W Family across from RR tracks

Scrap Family watches from telephone wires

Willy caches a nut for later

CT Parker shows off his misalined tail

Fodderwing and his crusy white elbow patches

Braveheart picks at broken sparrow egg on author's deck

Crows gather on beach before settling in surrounding roost trees

Crow enclosure at Riverside Nature Center

Bandy places stick in his peanut shelling spot

G / 3 eavesdrops on a conversation

Other is frightened by a blue jay feather on cage floor

Bandy steals penny from G / 3

Barb scratches Jo Jo

It was spring and time to start the secretive nest-building process all over again. Wilbur and Winona could be seen in the distance preening each other and bowing. Crows in the area were carrying large sticks or picking at the trees to break off the perfect piece. Fortunately, the events that year would not alarm me as they had last year. If the W's suddenly disappeared again, I decided I would focus my attentions on the Scrap family. If I was lucky, I might even discover the location of their nest.

As if on cue, the W's began snubbing me. I saw one of them over by the railroad, and he refused to come near me. At first, I wanted to believe it was just Winona being her usual stuck-up self, but then I saw that the Scraps had been the only ones coming for breakfast. They made themselves at home on the roof once again and landed in the garden unchallenged.

In fact, a few mornings in a row, I caught two of them underneath the kitchen window. I couldn't tell what they were doing there or what would interest them so close to the house. I could only guess that they had been picking at some loose concrete and eating it. I knew that crows and other birds ate small stones sometimes to aid in digestion. Mostly I was happy they felt they could forage safely in my garden.

One morning I identified Fodderwing for the first time in many months. I had heard his hoarse call in the distance recently, but until that point, I had never been positive that I had seen him in the garden. From the kitchen window, I saw him rummaging around on the ground under the birdbath. I recognized his signature crusty elbows. What was he looking for? Had he previously cached something there? His sharp eye spotted some dog fur I had brushed out and tossed into the yard last summer. It was partially covered with rotting leaves, but nonetheless, he found it. Did he think it might be a dead rabbit? He picked at the fur and finally pulled it all out into the open, but surprisingly, he didn't take any when he flew off. It would have made a nice lining for a nest, I thought, and a good find even if he was disappointed that it was not a dead rabbit. Perhaps he had gone home to check with his mate: "Honey, would wet dog fur be of any use in our nest?"

True to form, the W's threw me a curve ball. They stopped avoiding me and came into the garden for nuts one morning, all three of them. Perhaps the change this year would come in waves, mimicking the sporadic rhythms of the season. In the garden I saw Wilbur, Weagle, and Waif—as this youngest had continued to visit intermittently. I would have been surprised to see Winona there; she hadn't had the nerve to try her luck in the garden. Earlier in the morning, the Scraps had taken their breakfast unchallenged, even though the W's had seen me come out and leave the food for them. Later, while I was taking out the garbage, Wilbur flew over my head cawing and leading me back toward the park. Following him to his perch, I offered him some nuts as he flew over my head, the proximity of his wings almost lifting my hair like a breeze. I would have to wait for time to reveal whether the W's behavior signaled a permanent change or a passing aberration.

In mid-April, the shift in fact did take place. The W's had lived through one nesting season with me and thus had quelled any fears they might have had about my trustworthiness. I began to believe that their disappearance during nesting was driven more by the logistics of their chosen site. Perhaps it was located too far away for an easy commute.

Right before Wilbur and his clan stopped visiting me on a regular basis, a crow extravaganza took place in the garden. As I was passing the kitchen window with a plate littered with the remains of tacos I was too full to eat, a thought occurred to me. What if I set this plate on the deck, in the place where the crows were used to gathering up their nuts? It certainly would be less messy than trying to throw soggy foodstuffs onto the roof. I had nothing to lose, so I set out this first of many "crow plate specials."

To my extreme delight, the crows accepted the idea immediately, and I had five crows in my yard at once. But even more unexpected was the mixture of Scraps and W's eating peacefully together. One crow was standing in the pond, on the edge of the thawing ice, dipping his taco chip in the water as another watched from the bench. Two more crows were sharing from the plate, while the fifth—a pioneer of sorts—was the first crow to ever land on a branch of my young crab tree, which had finally grown large enough to support the weight of the one-pound bird.

Would I be sorry I had invited these messy eaters into my garden? Would they turn the pond into a soupy slough with their dunking habits? Would they eventually figure out a way to catch and eat my fish? I didn't care about these things as I watched the crows interact with each other and imagined the unique pictures I could snap. When they had departed, I collected a plate picked clean—save for the tiny bits of tomato the crows had carefully set aside.

But as suddenly as the ritual had begun, it ended. The crows decided they no longer wanted to come to the deck to eat. I noticed the absence of the W's in the morning, and the Scraps resumed their habit of waiting for me on the telephone lines. The crows would watch me put the food out in the morning, but I would return home to find it was still there, untouched.

A few theories came to mind. One possibility was that they were afraid of the shiny pie plate I had begun using as their dish. I had observed the crows approaching the plate and jumping back quickly, or grabbing a nut from it and flying off in a rush. Perhaps whatever hormonal surges drove their secretive behavior during nesting had kicked in, making them more wary of risky things, like descending into the garden. Perhaps the Scraps had been comfortable coming into the garden when they saw the W's do it, but since the W family had gone, they may have been less sure of the arrangement. Also, the composition of the Scrap family may have shifted, with a set of less confident sub-adults making up the morning breakfast club. They might appear reticent but really be less bold without the protection of their elders. Or else they might be less familiar with the protocol for securing the food. The original breeding pair of Scraps may have been occupying a different part of the territory, so I may have been looking at an entirely new set of birds. The Scraps had only recently begun reasserting their dominance in the garden, and I found that I couldn't tell them apart very easily, if at all.

Even after the W's had officially left for the season, I still had a few intermittent visits from them. Once Wilbur stopped by the roof for breakfast, and a few times Weagle came along. The yearling crow, finding himself outnumbered by the Scraps, was reserved and left without taking his share. The W family remained tamer toward me than it had been last year at this time and continued to be friendly during these occasional visits. When Wilbur could slip away from his duties to meet me at the park, he seemed harried and wary of the Scraps, who were at the ready to dive-bomb him, making it clear he was no longer welcome anywhere around there. On one occasion, I was able to talk with him before he had to rush off. "How's everything going? Have you been busy?" I whispered from below his perch. He let me quite near, and I could see the crease in his breast feathers indicating his paunch—evidence of our shared fondness for junk food. He barked at me in an excited way, as if to answer my question. But I was certain I didn't know the half of his adventures. I wished I could share more than a small snapshot of his world.

In late April, I caught sight of Wilbur once again, and I was shocked to see he had lost his tail feathers for the second year running. The reappearance of this condition convinced me that it was a yearly hormonal occurrence or a molt abnormality, not damage from a marauding predator, as I had first imagined.

As I rejoiced at the advantage of this visual marker, I fretted over Wilbur's handicap and wished him Godspeed as he navigated the next few months without his rudder. One exquisitely balmy spring Saturday brought another kind of lift to my heart as I sat on the deck enjoying the beginning of a fine season. It was Wilbur cruising by the garden at low altitude, as if he had come to say hello, knowing I would be out on such a day. I could see he had no intention of stopping, but he did make a point of looking me right in the eye as he passed, perhaps giving in to a feeling of homesickness. I had the impression he was flying in a big circle, and going right back home.

Meanwhile the Scraps had renewed their avid interest in bunny hunting. My garden was the focus of this activity, and although it was difficult to watch the crows behave so brutally, I accepted it as part of nature. I couldn't quite feel glad that they were thinning the population of garden moochers, thereby saving my plants from certain destruction. The catalyst for this latest hunting season had occurred when my neighbor's dog disturbed a nest of baby rabbits. The rabbit mother had naively placed them in the yard of an inquisitive canine. The crows seized upon this opportunity and carried off two tiny, cute little bunnies by their tiny, cute little ears.

It broke my heart to watch the rabbit mother's distress and hear her cries of sorrow and pain as the swooping crows with their sword-like beaks destroyed her life's work. The intense look in the eyes of the crows as they stalked around the roof, cocking their heads for a better look, waiting for the right time to snatch up the innocent rabbits caused me to romanticize them a little less. I respected them nonetheless as clever creatures that were only doing as nature intended. It made sense within the scheme of things that this healthy food source would be so abundantly available at a time when the newly hatched young crows would need it most.

The Scraps spent vast amounts of time checking and re-checking rabbit nest sites in my yard, hoping for another opportunity to grab a hapless youngster. The mom who inhabited my garden seemed a little smarter than average. I spied her jumping into the air to chase off the crows, and she kept moving around trying to fool them into believing her nest was elsewhere. But I was sure they knew exactly where it was—under the bridge by the pond, where it had been for years. For her young to succeed, they would have to learn the first rule of survival: if your mother tells you to stay hidden in the nest, *do so*!

Although it was our second baby season together, the Scraps never seemed to warm to me in the same way as the W's and the Parkers had. Was their behavior a function of their personalities, heredity, or ingrained beliefs about humans? Why had I been able to tame the other two families when, given the same amount of time and degree of interaction, the Scraps still viewed me with jaded suspicion? My loyalty remained with my original family as I awaited their return.

Although I continued to feed the Scraps faithfully, it was difficult not to take their resistance personally.

An unsatisfying but cordial relationship with the Scraps only made me miss the W family more. Try as I might to follow the Scraps to their nesting sight, I was unsuccessful. They had a good laugh at my expense one afternoon when, after figuring out that I was tailing them, they stopped and perched, waiting for me to catch up. When I finally did catch up, they flew off again, sometimes doubling back to where I had just been, causing me to walk in circles.

While the Scraps frustrated me in all ways, my relationship with CT Parker continued to blossom. He had become a shinning constant in the unstable breeding season. He always had time for me, even when the other crows were too preoccupied with nesting to appear.

He watched for me from a distant perch, so distant in fact that I could not make out his black shape in the trees. But he appeared when I did, circling low over my head to let me know he had arrived. Our time together was unique. CT was unlike other crows in his style of eating and caching nuts: while most crows gather up nuts while they are still in the shell and cache them for later use, he opened each one, swallowed the nutmeat, and held it in his antelingual pouch. CT worked this way until his capacity overflowed, and the nuts spewed forth from his pouch. Still he tried to gather and crack more, waiting patiently for me to toss him another from my post a few feet away. When the ground was not frozen or too cold, I was usually seated, my dog's leash wrapped tightly around my wrist, shortening her range and making her impatient with all this crow nonsense.

When finally CT became convinced that he could carry no more, he flew off toward the railroad tracks. His parting was always abrupt and belied our close bond. Sometimes, if the larder was getting low, he would return once more to repeat the process. I wondered why he preferred to shell his nuts before caching them. He may have figured out that he could stow a larger volume this way or it may have just been his personal style.

CT's curiosity about me showed itself one day when I brought a new camera to the park. It is always difficult to introduce new things to birds, and, fearing a loss of their trust, I am hyper-alert to anything that might upset them. Our friendship is more important to me than a few pictures, so I rarely push the envelope. In this vein, I had brought the camera to the park not to photograph crows but to experiment with other subjects.

CT spotted me, of course, and, after feeding him, I went about my business. He followed me to a grove of trees, at first wary of what I was doing with this strange new device but watching closely. When his nerve grew stronger, he perched on the limbs of the trees as I photographed the texture of their bark. When I felt he could tolerate it, I casually and as non-aggressively as possible pointed the lens in his direction. Spooking a little, he retreated to a higher branch. My selfish nature got the best of me, and I squeezed off a few frames of my beloved bird. The resulting failed frames show a black silhouette, with the telltale purple fringe of this new digital technology.

In time, CT began to accept the camera with greater ease. One chilly, windy March day, he posed for the cover of this book. Unbeknownst to both of us, his feathered form captured on that day would not only epitomize the beauty I saw in crows but would become the symbol of how close I had been able to come to these wild birds. It would become my most treasured crow photograph of a most treasured crow.

CT's gentle personality remained intact as he grew to adulthood. As he reached his first year, the inside of his mouth had yet to darken, retaining its red baby lining. He was a quiet crow, rarely uttering any sound in my presence, even when the rest of his family was calling wildly about some unseen event. He was a follower at heart and appeared to be living on the fringes of his family group. The very fact that he was the only crow to visit me on the many days when the others were busy either building, tending, or helping at the nest led me once again to believe he was unique in crow society.

Was he included in the duties of the nest? Or, was his time for me a result of ostracism by his group? During this period, he seemed nervous at times, but his relationship with me did not change in any significant way.

When the time finally came, baby Scraps followed their elders to the garage roof, and I waited eagerly for the return of the W's. Indeed, the day came when they introduced me to two more fledglings from another successful nest. I name these new W's Wally and W4. There is no sign that Waif and Weagle have had any part in caring for this new generation. But their disappearance did not preclude a continuing relationship with the family that might have been taking place outside my range of view.

I received a bittersweet visit from Waif and Weagle soon after the W family returned to reclaim their off-season territory. I heard Waif's familiar call—a sing-song warble—and dashed to the window in time to see him perched on the top of the garden bench like a confident teenager. He was calling repeatedly, and I could only assume it was to get my attention, since he was in my yard. As I raced out to feed him some nuts, I found Weagle perched atop the telephone pole. It was clear, however, that they had not come for food but perhaps just to visit and let me know they were well. After seeing me briefly, they flew off together in obvious good spirit, soaring up and down as though on a roller coaster.

It was apparent early on that the W's return this year would be different. The Scraps were stubborn about giving up their space, and it was clear they would not acquiesce easily. As a consequence, I was able to spend less time interacting with the W's, as the fight over territory lasted the whole summer. With neither group dominating the roof, the relaxed, carefree days of Wilbur teaching the little ones in my presence were gone. I met Wally and W4 at the park and in that environment could note little about their personalities. W4 was an extremely small bird, and Wally seemed more independent, sometimes absenting himself from the family even at this young age.

The W's had returned later this year, and I attributed this delay to the Scrap family's resistance to give up the territory. Although I did not like this turn of events I was interested to observe how it would resolve. I seemed to have created an artificial landmark in a territory that had never been disputed in the years since I had lived there.

Over twenty crows had now accepted me, including the Parkers, the Scraps, the Courts, the W's, and their immediate families. The park was dotted with their black shapes, and the sky came alive at my arrival. So clear was the delineation between the groups that I could easily have drawn corresponding chalk marks on the ground. No crow dared to breach this arrangement by accepting a nut from me beyond its family's range. It was only the W's who circled my head, marking me as theirs for all to see. They waited for me after I passed their area, and from the high trees they watched as I ran the dog in the tennis courts. They had a double dip of nuts as I passed them again on my return to the garden.

Mid-December found W4 and Wally remaining with their parents as the four of them continued visiting their territory around my home. W4 was the smallest of the four and had become tamer toward me over time. Very competitive with the other W's over food, he would race over to snatch nuts in an aggressive fashion.

In contrast to last year's babies, W4 and Wally did not disperse or join up with a winter flock. Was it due to the sex of the young or another factor? Had the encroachment and insistence of the Scrap family influenced Wilbur and Winona to allow the young birds to stay? Could they have been trying to even up the sides and thus remain strong competition for this favored area?

The W's had developed an intimidation tactic that I dubbed "the windmill effect." During the inevitable morning skirmish over possession of the garage roof, a Scrap would land boldly to take up his share. All at once, one angry W crow after another would swoop at him in rapid succession. It appeared that victory would be won through intimidation, persistence, and perceived threat. None of the Scraps were ever directly attacked or hurt, and if they could withstand the avalanche of force directed at them, they were rewarded with the food they desired. On some occasions, it was the W family that retreated in defeat, only to be victorious the next day. It felt to me, however, as if they were losing ground and that we would never return to the idyllic first days when we had first discovered each other.

In late January, I witnessed actual combat between the two families. The W's were the aggressors this time. Two of them ganged up on one lone Scrap, first chasing him and then tussling in the air with him, foot to foot. The event happened so quickly, I was lucky to have seen it at all. Over before it had started, the aftermath was more dramatic than the slight skirmish that had occurred. Appearing to defend their comrade, the Scraps gathered in Winona's tree, screaming in alarm. They were focused on something on the ground. Hurrying out to investigate, I found a single crow feather below them. Most likely, it had been plucked during the scuffle in the air. I wondered how this feather could have caused such a ruckus. With the crows still screaming, I carried the feather inside, hoping to calm them as I pondered the reasons behind their behavior.

Was it a fear of death or injury? I assumed crows had witnessed these things before and had seen mangled pieces of bird on the ground. Some of them may have even torn up other birds themselves and thus correctly interpreted the sign of a broken bird. Was there a taboo against crow-on-crow violence, giving this feather a deeper significance in crow culture? Several moments later, the crows still seemed deeply upset by the incident.

In fact, the rally was so intense that it summoned crows from the surrounding area. I counted fourteen birds that had come in support. Their cries diminished over time, and eventually the reinforcements dispersed. After the storm had calmed, one visiting crow gave a member of the Scrap family a poke on the head as he took his leave. It was not so much a violent gesture but rather an annoyed lunge, as if the bird were saying, "You called me over here for nothing!"

Would the combat resolve the issue of the roof? I did not have to wait long for my answer, as the next morning brought more of the same. All seven of the Scrap family waited for breakfast on the wire; they descended to the roof, cawing all the way, as if to ward off the W's. Instead, the spoils went to the W's, three of whom were able to chase the Scraps away, while the fourth casually gathered up the pizza.

In late February, I had a few days off and was able to spend some daylight hours at the park. During the week it was mostly empty of humans, and this state of affairs allowed me to try an experiment I would have preferred not be seen. Although I often talked to the crows in a low voice, I had never tried imitating their calls to see how they would react. I surveyed the area for passersby before unleashing my best crow imitation in the direction of my unsuspecting birds.

I'm sure many people have tried cawing at crows, mostly in jest and never to birds with whom they had shared long-standing relationships. I am unaware of anyone who has tried to talk with crows in their own tongue. That day in the park I was surprised to find that my attempts were answered, although I remained clueless as to the meaning of the conversation. I noted that the crow who answered me usually called back in a higher register than what I had come to recognize as a crow's natural sound. I wondered if the crow was imitating the higher pitch of my voice and thus acknowledging my signature. Was the crow helping me shape my own signature call, the marker of my identity? I wondered what the crows thought of my sudden imitation of them. Were they surprised that I was able to caw? Would they try to teach me how to do it right? Could I learn anything about their communications in this way? CT was most receptive to my attempts and broke his usual silence to talk with me.

The demands of a new job precluded me from continuing to talk with the crows in this way, and before I knew it, nest building had begun again in earnest. I first noted nest-building behavior on March 7 that year, when I wrote down that I had seen a crow carrying a stick in the park area. Several weeks later, I woke to find the front lawn littered with broken maple tree branches. The twigs were approximately twelve inches long and the diameter of a finger. At first, I suspected the recent windstorm, but other thoughts came to mind when, later, I saw four Scraps breaking the branches and picking at them with their beaks.

About this time, the W's relinquished control of the roof and begin their disappearing act. In early April, I caught sight of Wilbur and found that he had once again lost his tail feathers, a yearly event that I now thought of as marking the coming of spring.

The season would show itself as the year of the Scrap family, and I resigned myself to their dominance and tried once again to learn more about them. One of the younger members of the group, a bird from the past year's clutch, had distinguished himself enough to earn a name. I called him Braveheart, due to his bold nature and willingness to approach me while I was in the yard. He tended to wait for me to return from work, along with a few of his cohorts, and on such a day he surprised me with an act that reinforced his moniker.

Each day as I entered the house through my back door I made a habit of leaning over and speaking to my parakeet as he clung excitedly to his cage bars, happily greeting me after work. He had a view of the garden, as did I as I talked with him about the odd things a parakeet likes to hear. We were both startled and shocked when Braveheart glided toward us decisively, landing a foot away on the porch rail. He cocked his head at us, clearly curious about what we were doing. I was amazed to see him perched there looking through the window, without fear or pretense.

This lack of fear allowed him to linger long enough once to show me another side to his personality. Braveheart, as almost any youngster would be, was very fond of the orange cheese curls I had recently provided as snack. One morning I watched after putting out a leftover stew that coincidently contained similarly shaped carrots. The young bird scarcely hesitated over the bits of meat as he swooped in to confiscate an orange morsel. Gliding to the roof across the alley, he settled in to eat his breakfast, but, after taking a bite, he returned hastily with the orange imposter. Not content to simply abandon the offending carrot, he carried it back to the roof. Visibly crestfallen, he chose a small chunk of meat and retreated once again to his roof peak to eat. Suddenly, as though having a brainstorm, he returned to the roof, relocated the sinister carrot, hopped to the edge, and dropped it over the side. I could only conclude that in an altruistic way, he wanted to spare another crow the disappointment he had experienced over the orange fraud. I laughed and shook my head at the human quality of his disdain and his concern for his fellow crows.

Braveheart became a touchstone against which I could gauge my future observations of the Scraps. It struck me that a family of crows needed one bold member to spur them all to take greater risks, to push the envelope in their relationship with their environment. Up until this point, the Scrap family had been unwilling to cross an imaginary line, but Braveheart—like a catalyst for future change—had emerged to lead them in a direction they had appeared unable to take on their own.

PART II
Captive Crows

11

Riverside Nature Center

Many people, at one time or another, come across injured or orphaned wildlife. The first time I ever experienced this kind of situation was with a tiny wild rabbit I named Thumper. A cat roaming near my sister's yard had eaten Thumper's mother and siblings. My sister and I had no idea the proper thing to do in such a case, but, wanting to help, we "rescued" the rabbit and placed it in a small cardboard box. I was just out of high school at the time, and I never considered how the rabbit would learn to fend for itself if I raised it. I tried feeding it with an eyedropper, but my experiment as a wildlife rehabilitator was mercifully short for the rabbit, as he only lived about a day in my care. In those days, I had no idea that wildlife rehabilitators even existed.

In the summer of 2001, I was much older and somewhat better informed. A friend found an injured sparrow in his backyard and, knowing my love for birds, turned it over to me. Because English sparrows are not native to North America, most rehabbers here will not take them. Due to the abundance of needy wildlife, native and less common species are given first priority. Although the licensed rehab center I called would not take the sparrow, they did provide me with some instruction. The young bird had been gravely injured and was perhaps even semiconscious. Its head twisted uncontrollably to one side in rhythmic jerking motions. It had probably been the victim of another unsupervised house cat. I did not feel it could be saved, but neither did I want to leave it to suffer alone. I balanced the possibility of a quick end for the bird in the beak of a hawk against the rather slim chance that with a little darkness, rest, and protection it might recover. In the end my heart won out. Armed with the best advice of the wildlife rehabber and some soaked dog food on a toothpick, I tried my best to save the bird. The greatest pleasure of anyone who truly loves wild creatures must be to see the injured ones healed and set free to live the lives they deserve.

My latest foray into wildlife medicine, like the first, proved a failure. My charge died after only two days and protracted suffering. This episode led me to much soul-searching regarding the wisdom of tampering with the course of the bird's life. Would it not have been more merciful to allow a predator to take him in the night so that his suffering might be relatively short? Perhaps in my grandiose way I had believed it was better that he know someone had cared for him before he died. This catalyst led me to the Riverside Nature Center.

Chance and synchronicity played a large part in my volunteering at Riverside Nature Center. I would not have known the center even existed had it not been for the helpful intercession of one of my customers. Steve remembered a place that he used to visit as a child, a place filled with the orphaned and maimed, feathered and furred. I was still in the talking rather than the doing stage. My fear of change kept me stagnating, but Steve picked up the phone that day and made a few calls that would jolt me into action.

The next week, during my vacation, I set out to find this place Steve had talked about. Armed with maps and my hope for the future, I traveled down the busy unfamiliar streets that would lead me to Riverside Nature Center. I parked on the shady tree-lined street. It was with trepidation that I walked along the sidewalk to the entry, as I knew in my heart that this was more than a casual visit to a nature center to view wildlife. I was checking the place out for its possibilities and going against my shy nature, hoping to make a connection with a stranger who might further my goals. I was about to hold a fantasy up to the light and take a good look at it.

The big iron gates had been left ajar just enough so a body could pass through. It was late August, and the day smelled like summer heat, with an occasional accent of fox urine. The county forest preserves surrounded the center, and the trees cooled the crushed-stone path. I felt excited and exhilarated that such a place for wild creatures existed. The first large outdoor cage held a turkey vulture with its ugly bald head, specially designed by nature to keep the bird clean as it picked through decaying flesh. I rounded the soft curve in the path and stopped abruptly. Was it a mirage? Crows, they had crows! It was more than I had hoped for. Like seeing shoes in the store window that I must have, everything else became a blur, and a single desire crowded out all others. I knew I had to find a way to work with these crows. It was here that I belonged.

It was difficult to see the crows, as they were set against a large curtain of shade cloth. I imagined that the cloth was used to shelter the birds from the weather. Two large containers held food and water. The food dish contained what appeared to be raw meat, dog kibble, and a few slices of apple. I strained to make out how many crows were inside the enclosure and what they were doing. Sand had been used as a substrate at the bottom of the metal cage. One stout tree branch ran horizontally across the structure, forming the main perch, and a small bare tree was affixed in an upright position. Two wooden boxes, one high and one low, were provided also. Another high perch was tucked off in a corner, and when I craned my neck to see, I found one of the birds resting on it.

Where else might I have been afforded such a close look at this elusive bird? Here, they could not fly away from me, and I could observe their every movement. I stood there in front of the enclosure—not even a muscle twitching—my mouth slightly open in dumb wonder. The crows ignored me, going about their daily lives, used to being stared at by strangers. One cawed and twitched his wing feathers nervously from the main perch. Another crow dug in the sand, uncovering previous caches. I saw three captive crows that first day, and immediately my heart was lost to them.

I tore myself away from the crows to see what else I could find. A few hawks, an owl, squirrels, raccoons, and a pacing fox occupied the remaining outdoor pens. My first impression of the outdoor runs was one of peace and solitude. A small native wildflower garden near a stone wall and some picnic benches seemed a perfect place to meditate. I imagined myself caretaker there, doing the menial tasks that needed to be done to keep things functioning. I knew it would not be glamorous to scrape poop from wooden perches, or serve up the dead mice that seemed to be a dietary mainstay, but I already felt honored to be in the presence of these regal creatures. I was most attuned to the birds, and there were even more inside.

The building where the staff worked looked more like a mansion that had been accidentally placed in the woods than a wildlife hospital. In fact, in a distant former life, it had been a boarding school for troubled children. What I thought was the main entry was locked, and when I finally found the side entry, I felt that I had entered a place I shouldn't have.

It was cool inside, and a unique combination of odors greeted me—like the smell of a natural history museum where many old specimens fight off decay, combined with old newspapers and fish. The foyer led to an unmanned reception counter, and on the right, a staircase led to the second-floor bird room. Were visitors allowed to look upstairs? I wondered as I ascended the staircase.

As soon as I entered the room, my vision tunneled to contain only the two crows housed in a chicken wire cage adjacent to some windows. The one on the right immediately began talking to me as I approached. "Awwwww, awwwww," was her strange attempt at cawing. She was like a crow with a hearing disorder. "Waaaaz uuuuup?" she continued. "Hello, hello, hello." I was inches from her massive beak as she hammered the well-worn wooden crosspiece of her cage. The force of her blows would have been downright intimidating had I not been so charmed in her presence.

The crow on the left was quieter and seemed docile. He was slightly smaller than the other bird and quite disheveled. His eyes were glazed the milky white of cataracts. Occasionally when the other bird would call excitedly, he would join in with a staccato laugh. It was obvious that both birds had been raised around humans.

I spoke to both crows quietly, taking in the rich detail of their feathers, feet, and beaks. I studied these birds with a jeweler's eye, trying to memorize every nuance so that I might reproduce them later in clay. Although their look was familiar, viewing them from this distance gave them a new dimension. I was so enamored of this sight that the sorrow of two strong creatures living in such a small enclosure never occurred to me. The two crows were separated by a chicken wire partition, leaving each of them only enough space to turn around and hop from one perch to the other.

When I finally woke from my trance, I noticed the other birds in the room. A pair of cardinals flitted about building a nest from newspaper strips, their calls sounding amazingly loud indoors. Inside the large enclosure they shared, a couple of finches flew back and forth and hung on the chicken wire. One very sad blue jay, missing one wing, sat forlornly at the bottom of his cage. He was very different from the noisy, brash peanut-stealing mischief-makers I knew. I spent some time with him, absorbing his sadness and wishing I could restore him to his former self. He seemed to have given up. Next to him, a pair of mourning doves scattered their seeds on the floor of their cage, making a mess of which a three-year-old could be proud. A screech owl hid in his box, waiting for the cover of darkness under which to attack the dead mouse left for his meal.

I stepped into another room where musty stuffed birds sat atop an old wooden cabinet. Their eyes seemed to plead with me for dignity. They had outlived their usefulness as representatives of their species and so had been relegated to this back room to rot. It was hard to believe they were more than an amateur's attempt at taxidermy. And now with age and the aroma of decay, they were little more than grotesque and sad. This room was obviously the junk drawer of the center. A long tank of neglected turtles, a chalkboard, and a few yellowed, outdated display boards were stacked in a corner.

When I went back downstairs, there was a harmless-looking girl at the front desk. I said hello and smiled, hoping she was friendly. I asked her what she knew about the history of the crows and why they were there. As she spoke, I was sizing her up to see what qualities a person lucky enough to work at the center might possess. I was disappointed when she seemed dull, not at all like an exuberant zookeeper on Animal Planet. Since she was probably only of high school age, I could easily excuse her lack of expertise.

She told a story about feeding the crows in the outdoor pen. It became obvious that she feared them. She said that some local wild crows had gathered in the trees one day as she walked along with the trays of food. They were set to swoop down at her she concluded. I knew the details of her story had to be inaccurate. I know that crows fear and avoid people. I was certain these wild crows had plenty of food choices in the forest and weren't so desperate as to attack a hapless young girl with a plate of dog food. I was disappointed by the girl's immature explanation and her lack of knowledge about the natural world. She had probably witnessed some form of crow meeting that had nothing whatsoever to do with her. Perhaps a hawk had been nearby and needed mobbing. As the girl spoke, I spied another person behind a glass window hustling about in what appeared to be the kitchen. Perhaps *she* was fond of crows.

From the girl at the desk I learned that the animals on display to the public would not be released due to some permanent injury or handicap. She called them "educational animals," as if schoolchildren paraded in and out on a daily basis absorbing facts about the native wildlife. The two crows upstairs, Jo-Jo and Ollie, were former pets and had lived at the center most of their lives. That they could talk made them favorites with the staff, although the girl had had complaints that they were "noisy."

I headed back outside to look around and spend more time with the crows. Out there I noticed another member of the staff bustling around an empty cage next to the resident hawk. I started a conversation with him by asking him about the crows. I liked Ben right away. He was soft-spoken and proud of the work he was doing. He had started at the center as a volunteer and worked his way into a paid position. He had a particular fondness for hawks and was preparing a cage for one that was about to be transferred from another more crowded facility.

Ben was friendly, open, and easy to talk to. He looked as if he belonged there—the wildlife rehabber in cargo pants from central casting. He had a sensible but not overly sentimental attitude about the profession. He was more sensitive than manly but also sturdy and capable, with sandy blonde hair. Only one detail seemed out of place, the slight scent of tobacco. I was surprised to find out that such a nature lover smoked. If I had not come across Ben that day, the outcome of my trip could have been disappointing, my memories of it filled with longing and the sense of missed opportunity. I felt comfortable enough with Ben to broach the subject of becoming a volunteer. He handed me the director's card. "John Chelsea," it read.

John Chelsea's card remained in the armrest compartment of my truck, along with my cell phone. At the right moment, I would use them both. At this point, I did not feel very confident at even getting the opportunity to volunteer. I was convinced that there were thousands of college students studying wildlife biology who were more qualified and worthy in line ahead of me. I also imagined Mr. Chelsea had been jaded by his experiences with a busload of past volunteers who had "loved animals" but did not realize that loving them also meant cleaning up their poop. Many well-intentioned volunteers had probably come and gone. Someday soon I would have to muster the will to drive over all those roadblocks in my imagination.

It proved harder to contact John Chelsea than, say, the president of the United States. After many false starts, I finally succeeded in getting the guy on the phone. I was surprised by how punishing it was to offer my services for free. My first ten-minute phone conversation with Mr. Chelsea was downright painful. I felt as though I were dangling in mid-air from a bungee cord.

Mr. Chelsea was extremely discouraging, not because the center did not need any more help, but because, he seemed to imply, no one in his or her right mind would want to do this work. He called it "hitting-your-head-against-a-brick-wall kind of work." I wanted to convince him to give me a chance. I feared I might say the wrong thing at any moment, and we might lose whatever fragile connection we had. He grilled me about any animal experience I might have. He grilled me about the work I did for a living. It was a deteriorating dance of words. I felt more like a defendant on trial than a person offering to scrape up animal poop for free. I wrestled a vague promise out of Mr. Chelsea that he would call me back before I hung up the phone exhausted.

A few days later, while I was struggling through the double glass doors of the vet's office with a nervous Sheltie twisting her lead around my legs, my cell phone rang. It was John Chelsea asking if I was still interested in volunteering at the nature center. I was astonished. We set up a time to meet that Saturday.

I struggled into Riverside Nature Center on Saturday accompanied by the music of my thumping heart. Squashing down my feeling of dread, I told the blonde woman at the front desk why I was there. We made small talk as she finished preparing a plate for the opossum housed in a small cage in the front lobby. Suddenly a dark haired man in a camouflaged hunting jacket appeared. "Excuse me if I don't shake your hand," he said by way of introduction, "but I was handling some old bird specimens that were unexpectedly smelly." After taking a moment to clean up, he led me to his office on the second floor.

It was a long and narrow room, with one wall covered by books in a glass case, some of which overflowed the shelves. The desk was cluttered with papers. The office might have been a large cloakroom during the building's former life as a school for wayward children. One window overlooked the grounds, which were mostly blue and green this time of year. The office was not comfortable, and the man in it did not seem to want to be there.

I sat on a squeaky old swivel chair. I was wearing a pair of brand new Nike shoes, as though it were the first day of school. The shoes signaled to me a new beginning and a time of learning. I wore a new watch I thought Jane Goodall would have picked. I was playing at being a scientist, perhaps as a way to fit in, perhaps as a way to become what I most admired. I was embarking in a direction and setting my course based on a back catalogue of books I had read about pioneers who studied the animals that fascinated them. And although I would never compare myself with the likes of Jane Goodall or Bernd Henrich, I idolized these people and wanted to be like them, if even in small ways. I had come here to be closer to the crows; learning about wildlife rehabilitation would be a side benefit.

My conversation with John Chelsea on that day took some strange and unexpected twists. At times, I felt as if I was his therapist listening to a litany of problems he had with his staff and his job. His diatribes gave the impression that he was unprofessional and immature. The experience was certainly unlike any interview I had ever had. John told me the history of Riverside Nature Center—what was most probably his interpretation of the oral history that had been passed on to him, as it is passed on in most work cultures.

A character named Miss Judy had headed up the rehab center for many years. She had been somewhat eccentric but loved by the community. She ran the place like a petting zoo, and John cringed as he described baby animals running freely so that children could interact with them. "Can you say lawsuit?" he interjected. By following her misguided heart instead of a more conservative and intellectual philosophy, Miss Judy had made a mockery of wildlife rehabilitation, according to John. More than once, her approach had caused head-butting with the Department of Fish and Wildlife. After Miss Judy's death, an incompetent director had managed the center until John was hired to straighten things out. John felt he gave the center legitimacy.

The goal of a center like this one, John told me, was to release as many animals as possible back into the wild, not to turn them into pets. Unfortunately, the success rate was extremely low. "Nature doesn't need our help," was John's credo. Ever the Darwinian, he felt it was ludicrous to patch up a creature dumb enough to get injured in its own environment, only to send it out to repeat the same maladaptive response or pass on its inferior genes to the next generation. Hand-raising baby raccoons and squirrels was another item on his list of futile activities. He concluded that a mammal bonded to humans was a bad mammal, forever viewing people as a source of food. Such a habit could lead to dangerous interactions with humans in the future. So even when the center succeeded in releasing an animal, John still felt they had failed. He explained that the center existed not to help wildlife but to help the *people* who found the wildlife.

Ingrained in the human psyche is the desire to help the injured, whether another human or a tiny orphaned opossum. It was the director's greatest consternation to deal with this aspect of his job. His attitude made me wonder why he would ever work at the center. He was a paradox, the person who most vehemently opposed rehabilitating wildlife running a rehabilitation center. He would have seemed more at home as a sharp shooter culling the deer population. Why would he leave that job for this one?

The staff seemed to be causing him fits, too. Most of them were old-timers who had seen the reign of Miss Judy and had lived through the embattled interim director's scandal. They felt they knew more about the way things should run than John did. Perhaps this conflict was at the root of the gossip John shared with me on that first day. He felt a need to show them who was boss, and therefore he blustered in a fierce way instead of laying out a vision of the future. There was no doubt in my mind that John's vision of the future would clash wildly with that of the long time staff's. His latest project was to change the way orphaned raccoons were raised here. He had developed a new protocol stressing harshness in raising wild animals. He would order cattle prods. Dazed, I nodded my head when John explained that kicking sand in a kit's face was the best method to ensure they would survive in the wild. They must fear humans, not approach them for hand-outs. In my heart I felt this cruelty was wrong, but I hadn't had sufficient time to evaluate what I was being told. I thought that perhaps I just didn't understand these things.

I respected John's views of the situation, and I learned quite a bit in the time we spent talking. I did in fact like him, although he and I were very different. In the same way I had learned from the crow hunters, I did not discard the information John shared with me. It only led me to dig deeper, to find out if other rational intelligent people in the field opposed the views he held.

He filled out his theoretical ramblings with gratuitous information about the staff. I learned much more than I wanted to about the personal lives of his employees. I would forever try to match up his descriptions with the people I encountered in this place, although I would have preferred to draw my own conclusions without his help. There were obviously some disturbing political conflicts going on at the center. It struck me as extremely odd that the director would share all of this information with me, only a potential volunteer. I had hoped to meet a scholarly mentor, and instead came away disillusioned by this flawed mortal.

My brand-new researcher's watch began to beep, and we both looked around for the source of the sound. It was a good stopping point, and John had deemed me fit to start my work as a volunteer the following Saturday. I shook the hand of the man who had given me my first class in wildlife rehabilitation.

I was giving up my Saturday morning, gulping down coffee in the car. This would have been my time to sit on the deck and reflect on my garden, and I missed that. Had I made a mistake committing to this early morning endeavor? I made it to Riverside with a few minutes to spare, just enough time to finish my coffee and slip through the black iron gate into a new world. I was to report to Jenny, the woman with whom I had been making small talk last Saturday. She smiled when she saw me through the lab window. She was a pleasant woman but not friendly. I sensed that she was not interested in knowing me, but perhaps in time the wall would come down.

I was in the back hallway, a space reserved for staff. I was expecting a clinical environment, but it was more like a garage sale. Metal stands used to store folded towels lined the halls. The towels were ragged, obviously donated castoffs. The area had a makeshift feeling. The air was filled with an unpleasant odor—a natural byproduct of preparing unappetizing meals for stinky creatures. I could hear a mammalian scurrying from a room full of metal cages.

Jenny led me around a corner made narrow by an assortment of junk lining the walls. She was introducing me to the "squirrel woman." Blond and maternal, she was nursing baby squirrels in her lap. Perhaps the cattle prods hadn't come in yet. This woman obviously cared as deeply for squirrels as I did for crows. She cooed over them as though they were the most beautiful creatures she had ever seen. Plastic carrier kennels, some with cute rodent faces peering through the grates, surrounded her. The room looked like a basement filled with junk.

Undaunted by the decor, I took my marching orders from Jenny. I would be working with Deb in the indoor nature center upstairs—where Jo Jo and Ollie lived! I was glad to hear I would be near the crows. Deb was the person who welcomed me on my first day. She was quite willing to share what she knew.

We started by preparing a cleaning solution of Nolvosan and water. First, we would wash down the cages, then scrape the perches, and supply fresh paper for the floors. The meals for the specific birds had already been prepared and set out on cafeteria trays. Deb and I talked while we worked, and it didn't take long to explain how my passion for crows had led me there. When she found out about my love of crows, Deb allowed me to work on Jo Jo and Ollie's cages.

Ollie, Deb told me, was a male crow whose health was deteriorating. He seemed frail and old. He strained to see the world through the white film of his cataracts. His feathers appeared messy and tattered. He had an extremely gentle way about him. Deb told me he spoke in French at times, but usually he only contributed his strange clown-like laugh when Jo Jo became raucous. Ollie tilted his head at me in a friendly way and emitted a soft mewing noise. I did not know if he was speaking human or Corvid, but he clearly expected this to be a pleasant encounter.

I worked at cleaning his cage to perfection while Jo Jo jumped from perch to perch next door. She seemed agitated and jealous. Jo had rudely pecked a few members of the staff, and I tried to discern a reason for her behavior by questioning Deb about her. I refused to believe she would be aggressive without a reason, and I assumed she did not like certain staff because of the way they acted around her. Perhaps they were too invasive inside her small enclosure, the only tiny place she could call her own, or perhaps she sensed their fear of her and wanted to press her advantage. Perhaps she simply did it to amuse herself and get a reaction. I felt sure she would not stab at me.

Deb gave Ollie his metal dish as I lay the fresh papers on the floor of his cage. She then held out one green grape, which Ollie took delicately from her hand. She stroked his head lightly, and he blinked with his nictitating membrane. I asked Deb if I could touch him as well, and when she nodded I reached out to stroke his head with my index finger. It was the first time I had ever touched a crow, and I would remember it always.

It was Jo Jo's turn next. Without the chicken wire between us she seemed bigger and more powerful. She looked fit enough to survive in the wild, had it not been for a wing injury that made it impossible for her to fly. As it was, she could barely jump from the floor of her cage to her lowest perch. I was sure her ability to relate to other crows had been severely retarded, as had her ability to figure out the basics of survival in the urban wild. Before the Migratory Bird Act made it illegal, she had been kept as someone's pet. She sat quietly near the rear of her cage as I worked. She seemed a queen expecting that this service should be performed for her. It hardly seemed work, setting her cage right for another day, and it was over all too quickly. As soon as we locked her back up, she began her signature rendition of, "Hello, hello. Whaaaats zuuuup?"

She serenaded us with her crazy laugh and occasional cawing to the wild crows outside as we continued down the row of cages. Her ability to caw like a normal crow was somewhat impaired and made her sound like a foreigner in her own tongue.

I tried to learn as much about the other bird residents of the nature center as I could, including the injuries that had brought them there. Most of Deb's answers were vague, but she was relatively new there also. "I think a head injury or something neurological," was her stock answer. Once the animal had been committed to the center as educational, it appeared not to matter why. If the staff proclaimed an animal non-releasable, it received nothing more than meals and a clean cage. No one seemed to ponder its injury any further. I was learning their attitudes and philosophy of the center itself.

When we finished the indoor cages, including that of the sad one-winged blue jay, it was time to go outside. We started with the cage of ring-billed gulls. Stepping inside the enclosure to rake the sand, I felt important again. As though holding a position sought by many, I proudly scraped and hosed, feeling, I was sure, the envious eyes of the passing visitors. Some asked us questions, and although I remained silent, I was thrilled to be on this side of the fence.

Deb once again kindly deferred to my interests, and although it was not next on the list, we moved to the cage of captive crows. I stood ready to enter the cage as Deb fiddled with the stubborn lock. I imagined how difficult this task would be in the grip of our frozen winters. It was dark inside the enclosure, shaded by the trees outside and the metal roof; it had a depressing feel for an outdoor cage. It smelled of wet sand and rotting wood. I took my first close look at the three crows. No longer boldly strutting about in the sand, the three of them huddled together on the highest branch of the bare-limbed tree that served as their furniture. I set to work scraping white splotches with my metal tool. There were two boxes affixed inside the cage to provide shelter from the weather. One was positioned near the ground, and the other was higher up, on the street side of their home. The wood felt damp and unfriendly to the bare skin. I couldn't imagine feeling comfortable inside one of the boxes during a storm. But crows are used to rustic conditions. We stole glances at each other, the crows and I. They peered at me with their closest eyes as I spoke to them in a soft voice. Deb had left me alone with them to go do other things. I could have stayed with them all day, had I not feared being thought of as the crazy crow woman. This was the same fear that had stopped me from carrying out so many of the experiments I have concocted.

I felt slightly wary passing under their perches, but it was not because I had not been this close to crows before. The crows I had interacted with were wild and free to fly away at will. These were trapped there with me, a virtual stranger. It was an artificial situation, and my crow sense was not free to play out its instincts. As I moved about, talking to them, we both loosened up a bit. At one point, as I was kneeling with my back to the group, one of the bolder crows flew to the ground and began to sneak up behind me. "You were going to try to steal my scraper, weren't you?" I teased him. He reminded me of my dog as a puppy, impishly making off with my shoe. He was comfortable enough with my presence to initiate a game, although he never did grab the shiny metal tool.

Deb returned with the crows' meal and slipped inside the cage. Another crow had come down to the main tree trunk perch that spanned the width of the cage. Deb handed me a grape. "Sometimes this one will take a grape from you. He's the friendliest towards people," she offered. I held the grape out towards the crow. Ever so gently, and with the air of concern that he might accidentally hurt me, he slowly took the grape from between my fingers. For a bird species accused of brutally pecking the eyes of a newborn calf, he certainly exhibited a courteous nature. Sometimes it is true that those with the most power (and the biggest beaks) feel the need to wield it the least. I thought of my own scrappy parakeet and the way he gleefully pinched my fingers, making me shriek in pain.

On my first day at the nature center, I had realized two of my fondest dreams: I had touched a live crow, and I had hand-fed one a grape. I went home feeling satisfied and excited. Still, my time as a volunteer sapped my energy. I was used to having my weekends to myself. I tried to think of working at Riverside as taking a class and tried to approach it with an eagerness to learn. But I found garnering any information from the staff slow going. Those who were willing to discuss things at length were either new or didn't have enough knowledge of wildlife to educate me. It surprised me that I knew more about nature and rehabilitation principals than some members of the staff. With each visit there, I saw less and less to impress and more and more to dismay.

I heard a few stories that troubled me, tainted as they might have been by the teller's perspective. Still I believed there must have been kernels of truth in each of them. I heard about an owl that had lived at the center for the better part of its life. One day the director decided to release him. So it was that in the late fall, with no actual plan for helping this owl survive in an environment that had become like foreign land to him, he was set free. After living in a small cage inside a warm room for years, they released him to fend for himself. He didn't last but a few days before his frozen body was found near the place he had been given his freedom. This story appalled me. How had the director expected such a creature to survive without any remedial training or practice at catching his own food? For years he had been served up the prison fare of dead mice and no longer had the physical power or muscle tone to catch his own live specimens—if in fact, he even remembered that he was supposed to. He had had no room to fly in his indoor enclosure, and suddenly he found himself at large, where flying was not a freedom but survival. I was no expert at release, but even I knew that was not the way to do it.

I had read about a technique called "soft release." The animal is kept in an outdoor pen and fed, and eventually, when it has been acclimatized, the door to the pen is left open. When the animal feels ready, it can leave, but it always knows its way back home to the meal waiting inside the enclosure, should it find itself in trouble. I was incredulous that people who rehabilitated animals for a living would not have considered such an option with the owl. I hoped that I was just missing a part of the puzzle and that the employee, who had disagreed with the release of the owl, had distorted the story. Furthermore, reputable rehab facilities would have access to a flight cage, which would allow staff to determine the ability of a bird to fly, as well as help the animal rebuild its muscles and flight skills.

The more Saturdays I spent at the center, sweeping up molted feathers and lining the cages with fresh papers, the more I found that unenlightened neglect was the general tenor of the place. The vet came in on Wednesdays, so pity the poor creature that was rescued on a Thursday, as it would have a long wait to be evaluated or treated. An information card was filled out with the help of the folks who brought the animal in, after which it was given a cursory exam by the staff, aimed mostly at determining if it should be put to death immediately. It was then placed in a cage with the appropriate diet for its species. The center was supposed to provide more care than an animal would receive if taken in by a well-meaning individual and kept in the basement. But in some cases, the basement would have been a better option, albeit an illegal one.

One Saturday soon after I started volunteering, I was informed that the next week I would be working with a volunteer who was a keeper at the zoo. Jenny said that this person was very knowledgeable about birds and that I could learn much from her. I looked forward to it all week—not only meeting a person who did such an interesting job, but hearing an intelligent overview and learning from the insights of an expert. Surely she would help me make sense of what I was seeing at Riverside. My imagination painted a picture of her as part Joan Emery and part kind veterinarian. We were introduced the next Saturday just as I was rising from tying my shoelace. "Glad to meet you," I smiled. A girl in her mid-twenties wearing rumpled clothing leaned against the wall, her long brown hair tucked behind her ears. The look on her face told me immediately that she had been unaware that she would be working with me today and that she was entirely displeased with the notion. I felt instantly rejected but tried to understand how she might have felt. I was never pleased myself when a bright-eyed trainee was foisted on me at my own job, so perhaps a similar attitude had caused her negative reaction. Maybe after she got to know me better, she would change her view.

We filled our buckets with disinfectant solution, and I trailed Kathleen upstairs. I tried to be charming and friendly, but she responded with curt one-word answers. I did manage to drag some conversation out of her, but after learning a few things about her, I took a different tack. Perhaps, I thought, I should just shut up, as she appears so annoyed at my chatter. While we worked quietly together, I thought about the things she had told me. She seemed to agree with John's views, and like him, she had a background in biology. She currently worked in the conservation department at the zoo, after having spent many years tending to an assortment of different creatures—including a stint in the birdhouse. She moved with confidence among the birds, and I admired that, although I did not admire her or her technique. She was gruff and showed no softness toward the birds at all. She treated them as though they were specimens and the center a project that needed cleaning up. She didn't bother to hide her disdain for the way the staff managed things there, pointing out their errors as we went. Her corrections were helpful to me, but they seemed to emanate not from a place of love or concern for living things but from a well of hate and anger toward the people who were so inferior to her. If the birds benefited from her ideas, did the source of the help matter?

She was especially rankled by a grackle with bumble foot. No one had bothered to give him the proper therapeutic perches or a soft surface to stand on. Ideally, his cage should have been cleaned twice a day, not once like the rest, because his leg injury forced him to stand in his own waste matter. His feet were coated in it, and Kathleen grabbed him roughly and began yanking and picking at them with a cloth soaked in disinfectant, as though he were a wooden bird. Had I been the grackle I might have preferred to languish there rather than be "helped" in this way.

When we reached the one-winged blue jay, Kathleen angrily chided him for "sitting like a lump." I'm sure this lifted his sagging spirits. It made me feel weak to talk to the birds when I was around Kathleen. Any dislike she may have instantly felt for me was quickly becoming mutual. I hid my feelings from her, treating her with a respect that I hoped would help me learn from her. As I worked with Kathleen, I thought about how a personality can change a plain-looking person into a beauty. But all I could remember about her face were the red splotchy pimples that looked as though she had scrubbed at them with all the anger she felt toward the world.

Kathleen's know-how and efficiency helped us finish our tasks early, so I went outside to see Deb and the crows. We stood near their cage talking about the world of wildlife rehabilitation. Apparently, a large part of the work centered on public perceptions of what the center should be about. A good part of the day was spent dealing with the unrealistic, overly sentimental public. Generally, people wished that wildlife issues would be resolved like Disney movies. As Deb and I talked, one of the crows flew over to me, grabbing the cage bars with her feet and landing inches from my head. I took this as a friendly gesture, and Deb commented on how unusual it was for the crow to do this. I noted that the green band on the crow's leg was stamped with the number thirteen. I began differentiating this crow from the others, calling her G (for green band)13.

I wish I could say that I looked forward to spending time at Riverside, but although I enjoyed being near the crows, I felt that I was wasting a large portion of my weekend. Kathleen was also weekly volunteer, and she did not grow to enjoy my company as time passed. She seemed to want the place to herself and so considered me a burden. I understood her viewpoint to some extent but was disappointed that events were taking this negative turn.

One week Kathleen decided the birds needed their nails clipped. Muttering under her breath about the staff who had allowed the birds to remain in this condition, she hurried off in search of some clippers. It was interesting to watch her handle the birds. I hoped that she would share with me her techniques for catching and holding the wild ones, but I had to be content with watching and learning. First, she grabbed the grackle with bumble foot, snipping away the excess nail and then releasing him to his home. Next, she attacked the cardinals. The pair of them had lived together for a number of years, and in the spring they built nests with paper towels in margarine cups to pass the time. Any eggs they laid would be destroyed, as it is against regulations to allow captive wild birds to breed. I wondered about the wisdom of using the same clippers on all the birds without disinfecting them in between, but I said nothing. What I did know was that I wasn't a trained zookeeper like Kathleen.

I was especially excited that next she was going to work on Jo Jo, the more aggressive of the two indoor crows. I secretly hoped Jo Jo would bite her with her powerful beak, but Kathleen was able to subdue the rambunctious crow. She placed Jo Jo in a cat carrier while she worked at mending a perch in her cage, securing the burlap twine binding that was beginning to loosen, causing a potential hazard for the bird. She explained how birds needed different surfaces and textures on their perches for the health of their feet. Again, I sensed that her commentary was coming from a well of haughty superiority. Maybe she could have done a much better job than any of the staff at the center, but I hadn't walked in their shoes and was unwilling to assume that I understood the spell of complacency they seemed to have fallen under. I did, however, agree that the birds' nails needed clipping.

I watched as Kathleen held Jo Jo and cut her nails. Her "calming" patter during this ordeal indicated her inner feelings, and they did not reflect deep concern for the bird. She spoke as though Jo Jo was her adversary, as though the bird was fighting her out of a sense of malice. She painted a self-portrait of her inner negativity by projecting the crow's motives. When she was finished, however, there was no denying the crow was more comfortable.

The week after Kathleen clipped the birds' nails, I got my first taste of death and loss at the center, when I returned to learn that both the cardinals and the bumble-foot grackle were dead. The grackle, it seemed, had been put out of its misery, a decision that had been rumored as far back as my first talk with John. There is a regulation that any bird who cannot perch shall be put to sleep. This grackle had been living on both borrowed time and the sentimental feelings of those at the center who cared for him. The cardinals' deaths were more mysterious; they had dropped suddenly, within a day or so of each other. I inquired as to whether there had been any attempt to find the cause, lest some infection be rampant or some mistake in husbandry the cause. "No," I was told. The staff was content to repeat to themselves that the birds were "just old." The second of the pair, they said, had probably died of heartbreak over the loss of its mate.

I was truly getting a sense that if I were an injured bird I would not want to die at the Riverside Nature Center. I'd rather die in the field with my boots on, maybe grabbed by a hawk, than be brought to this foreign environment and left to languish in a metal cage. I would prefer the whistle of the trees, perhaps even the fear of the dark of night, to the unfamiliar sounds of humanity and the disorientation of being abandoned with my food in a pile near by. The chances that any animal would be released from this place were slim, and the words of John Chelsea came back to haunt me, though not for the reasons he cited. I did not become discouraged at seeing the death of the majority of creatures brought in; I became discouraged at the lack of professional integrity and dedication toward the flood of injured that passed through the front entrance. I was beginning to think my time at the center would be fruitless.

I was thinking about discontinuing my volunteer work at Riverside one day as I swept the floor in the reception area. "My neglected floor at home needs sweeping," I lamented inside my head. Although I showed interest, there wasn't anyone there willing to take me under his or her wing. I had been reduced to learning what I could by reading the intake cards left on the desk. Fighting with Kathleen over rights to scrape poop off a perch ranked under the tasks I could have been doing at home.

On the last Saturday I spent at Riverside, I realized that Kathleen truly wished I did not exist, that her feelings were not the imaginings of my sensitive mind. My final encounter with her took place in the janitors' closet. I approached with a smile, a rag, and a bucket. A sour look crossed her face when I asked how she was. I followed her out of the closet a few moments later to catch the tail end of a conversation she was having with the boss, Jenny. "Just let me get beyond the finch cages, and then she can help me," she told Jenny. It was obvious she was lobbying so that she wouldn't have to work with me. I felt humiliated and wished I knew what I had done to cause this young woman to dislike me so intensely. I usually didn't have that effect on people. The rejection was official; nothing about it was covert anymore. My heart sank, and I felt embarrassed. I wished I could run out the door and flee from this place where I was not wanted.

"Well I guess there's been a change in plans, and I'll have you work in room two this morning," was Jenny's way of deflecting the exchange I had overheard. Room two was a hospital room where a robin kept as a surrogate parent for babies had been living. It also housed other temporary birds that would either be released or die there. I did my best to make their cages comfortable again, amidst the chatter of staff who knew each other and were at ease there. I was not. I did not receive much instruction on the procedures for this room and had to keep checking in for direction as if it were my first day on my very first job.

The highlight came when Jenny told me to "Move that duck, set up his cage, and then move him back." My heart thumped as I tried to imagine how I should accomplish this task without looking totally dumb and inexperienced. Swallowing my false pride, I asked Jenny, "*How* do I move this duck?" Throw a towel over him, she told me, and I realized I should have known the answer. I had done the same thing with my own bird at home, but I would have forgotten my name in the heat of battle. I got the job done, although quite indelicately for the bird. I was glad no one had seen my sputtering ineptitude as I had unglamorously grasped the charging, hissing duck by any part that was not wriggling. This turned out briefly to be his neck, as I tried to maneuver him without hurting. Finally, buzzing with adrenaline and pride, I secured my first charge in his clean pen and set about mopping the floor with disinfectant.

By this time Kathleen had finished her work upstairs, unhampered by me, and now had extra time to get into some trouble downstairs. I knew she had been lurking about when Jenny gave me my instruction regarding the duck. She decided this duck needed something, although I can't recall what, but he got away from her. Kathleen made a big show of chasing him about the center. "The duck escaped," she announced. I hoped that no one thought it was due to something I had done. I wondered briefly, paranoid, if Kathleen had set up a scenario to make it look as though the duck had escaped on my watch.

I decided then that the Riverside Nature Center was not a place I wanted to spend my time. I knew before I left that day that it was my last visit as a volunteer. I left partly because I wasn't learning anything and saw no hope of doing so in the future and partly because I did not want to become one of these people with their callous and necessary gallows humor. If working with injured wildlife would one day harden me to their plight, I did not want to do it. I left also because even though I was working near the crows and sometimes inside the cage with them, I had less time to observe them. I feared they would become like one of the tropical plants on my accounts, a part of a job, whose beauty many times escaped me. I could not tolerate that happening with my crows, and so I left with no intention of ever returning.

During that next week a tiny seed of a plan germinated in my head. What if I returned to the center for some work of my own, taking advantage of the fact that there were three captive crows available for unlimited observation? What might I learn about crows in such an intimate setting? My brief stint as a volunteer had opened up this new inroad, and I decided to return to the center for my own purposes. This decision began a year-long weekly observation that would give me new perspectives on the American crow.

12

Jailbirds: Creative Crows in Captivity

The weather was already turning cold that first day as I stood beside the enclosure observing. I was a little nervous about attracting too much attention with my notebook and tape recorder, especially since I hadn't told the center that I was not going to return as a volunteer. Since none of the other volunteers showed up on a regular basis, I felt I would not be missed anyway, and I used this rational to avoid the uncomfortable phone call I preferred not to make.

My first order of business was to discover a system for reliably telling one crow from the other. I also had to develop a strategy for taking useful notes on the fly. Gloves wouldn't work, so I had to rely on my pockets to keep my hands warm between scratches on my note pad. I decided on this first session to write down everything I saw as best I could. I named the crows out of necessity, without much thought toward the future. One of the crows was missing the green leg band that the birds wore, so I called him Bandy in my notes. While still a volunteer I learned Bandy had a talent for removing the plastic ring. I had already informally named G13, on that day at the side of the cage, although I could not pick her out right away. By default, the last bird became Other. As I began to know the birds, I regretted cavalierly calling that bird Other, and I tried to change her name many times. Nothing ever stuck, however, and the odd name became more fitting as time passed. In my heart and thoughts, her name became just as endearing as any pet's name could have been. For what is a name but a handle by which we grab the essence of a person or animal?

In the beginning, it was extremely difficult for me to follow the crows' frantic actions and keep track of who was doing what. I started every session by orientated myself to who was who, and once this detail was out of the way, my observations began to make more sense. I also developed names for the various areas of the cage.

After several weeks of watching these captive crows, I began to see the clear distinctions between them. It was obvious they each had a different personality as well as a different focus within the group.

Upon close inspection, the birds differed visually. Bandy had the largest beak, and once I knew this about him it became obvious immediately upon seeing him. He also had one errant feather that stuck out of his right wing at an odd angle. I would never know the sex of the individual birds; however, I developed hunches based on the group dynamic, and, right or wrong, I organized them that way in my mind. I felt Bandy was a male crow and the other two females.

G13 was a people-oriented bird, as evidenced by her willingness to interact with me. She began an endearing habit early on of greeting me by flying to the cage bars nearest to me as I walked up and settled in for my observation. It was clear that she enjoyed human company. She also followed me as I left, learning the meaning of the word *good-bye* the second time I used it. She was a gracious hostess—without fail she greeted me, and when I was ready to leave, she walked me to the door. She was just a shade smaller than the other two crows in the cage and appeared squatter when on the ground. Although I recognized her as an individual even before I left my volunteer post, during my observation I noticed a quirk that helped me pick her out of the pack of look alikes. She tended toward nervousness, I think, and was almost constantly flicking both her wings and her tail. When I found the bird with this habit, it was easy to then identify the other birds as well. At certain points, I wondered if G13's constant flicking could be due to a physical abnormality. It seemed more pronounced than in any other crow I had ever observed.

Then there was Other. Ironically, the name fit her in more ways than one, as her place in this threesome, whether by choice or pecking order, was odd man out. She hung back from the other two and rarely solicited attention from her bird companions. She was the least likely to pay humans any mind, flying to the highest perch whenever they entered her enclosure. She may have been an extremely shy bird or one that had never fully adjusted to her captive life. It was also possible that she was chronically ill and for this reason was less involved. This is not to say she never interacted with her cage mates, only that, if given the choice she preferred to spend much of her time alone.

Observing these crows so closely, closer than I was able to get in nature, convinced me that in fact every crow is slightly different. With a powerful enough lens, it could be possible to differentiate crows in the field if one had the patience. Beaks especially were fertile ground for comparisons, as anomalies are common. For example, G13 had a slight crossbill: the tips of her upper and lower beak were crooked when it was closed. It struck me that crows' beaks could be used in the same way as the scars on dolphin fins, to identify individuals in a group.

Crows can tell each other apart, in my opinion, because as science has shown, birds can see light in the ultraviolet range, making colors available in this spectrum that are invisible to humans. It is possible that an all-black bird like a crow has unique markings that fluoresce, giving it a visual identity not visible to human eyes. Experiments done with finches under controlled lighting indicated that females responded less favorably to males when special glass that cut ultraviolet light was placed between them. Birds see the world much differently than we do.

While still a volunteer, I was privy to the files of the captive crows. I was curious as to what had brought them to the center in the first place. Each file consisted of a sheet of paper with a one-line entry listing the admission date, injury, and band number. The numbers listed in the crows' files did not match up with the bands on the actual birds. Perhaps the original bands had been lost or damaged and replaced over time without anyone noting the new numbers in the files. Perhaps—and more likely—the center had lost track of which birds they had. The files indicated that the three outdoor birds had been admitted in August of 1994, September of 1997, and May of 1998. Staff recollections regarding which bird matched which file proved unreliable. One of the three had had a broken wing, another a right foot injury, and the remaining one was categorized as a former pet.

I made some early guesses of my own and then changed my mind over time. It was possible that G13 was the former pet, as evidenced by her ability to bond with people. Conversely, Other could also have fit this profile if she had had a bad experience as a captive and consequently no longer trusted or wanted anything to do with humans. All three crows seemed robust and visually appeared no different from any of the wild crows I knew. They all made normal sounding vocalizations and seemed to do so at appropriate times. Looking normal inside of a cage, however, did not translate to being releasable, I admitted. The former pet especially might not have the skills to survive in the wild. However, I did inquire as to whether the birds had ever been reevaluated for possible release. The people I asked shrugged their shoulders and offered vague comments in response to my question. In the long run, I supposed it didn't matter what injury or handicap had brought the crows to Riverside, and I ceased pondering the issue.

Many questions drove me to continue visiting with these three, despite the time of year and the approach of inclement weather. How did they spend their time? What was their relationship with each other and with the world around them? Were they happy in captivity? Would they behave like normal crows in this unnatural environment? How would their vocalizations in the cage differ from or be similar to those I had heard in the wild?

Captive crows left to their own devices, provided full-service meals but no gainful employment, had ample opportunity to either languish in a depressed way or make use of their time in the pen. These three chose the latter option. While their neighbors the owl and the hawk waited listlessly for their daily dead mice, the crows were active and engaged.

They called often during the day, and this behavior allowed me to hear some unique sounds. The crows' vocalizations fell into some predictable categories. I cannot say whether these were natural crow sounds or combinations of sounds they had heard while living among people. One such sound I dubbed "boing." It seemed a cross between a hiccup and a cluck. The first time I heard it I was not sure if it had been a crow or some mechanical noise in the distance. The sound of a drop of water falling onto the top of a metal drum might approximate this call. It wasn't crow-like or mammalian. The caller produced it by bending at the neck and jerking upwards. Most often made in doublets or triplets, the sound could be repeated many times over at varying intervals. I once heard it repeated twenty-five plus times within one half hour. For reasons unknown to me, only Bandy and Other ever made this call.

I speculated that the call was non-aggressive and related to food or feeding activities in some way. On at least three occasions, Other made the boing call just before descending to the ground for food. In another instance, after Bandy had uncached a nut and carried it to a perch to eat, Other decided to search the sand for something to eat as well. Bandy came down to the ground and sidled up next to Other while making this boing sound. The call was quite purposeful and had obvious meaning and intent. Had the nut Bandy had just eaten been Other's? Were the two communicating about the food or cache spots in some way? Could this call be used in situations of friendliness, as a way to diffuse any ruffled feathers?

I made extensive use of a mini disc recorder to capture the sounds made by the crows during my observations. They correlated with the notes I took and later deciphered at home. The recordings allowed me to match up calls with the crows who had made them and with whatever activities had been going on at the time. I experimented with the crows by playing their recorded voices back to them from my laptop computer. Once I played Bandy making his boing call. Only Bandy showed the slightest acknowledgement of the sound, perking up slightly and looking in the direction of the sound. I played the call several times to the apparent disinterest of the other crows. Approximately five minutes later, Other made the boing call, and then descended to the ground to eat an egg that Bandy had discarded earlier. Moments later Bandy took a piece of meat to the doorway area, planted his feet in an almost ritualized way, and sounded the boing note. Would these events have happened without my introducing the sound from my computer?

During another observation, I played the sound of G13 cawing what I would classify as contact notes. Again, Bandy was the one who showed the most visual reaction. He became agitated and began flying around the enclosure, looking skyward for the crow who was calling. I played it several times, and although he could tell it was coming from my direction, he seemed unable to locate the crow responsible for it. G13 meanwhile continued walking about in the sand, and Other sat unperturbed on the highest perch of the main tree. After a gap of about thirty minutes, I played the call again. Bandy reacted in a similar fashion, flying about agitated as if he believed it were a real crow. He searched the sky for a bit before settling on his favorite perch and calling, "Kuk kaa, kuk kaa." (Come here, come here.) G13 also reacted to this second call with wing and tail flicks, and when Bandy called out, she called out with him. It was hard to judge whether she was reacting to Bandy's calls or to the recording. In either case, it was interesting to wonder if the crows were unable to recognize individual voices, as the recording had fooled them so easily. If they recognized G13's specific voice and could see she was not making the sound, how would they reconcile these conflicting factors? It could be argued, however, that recording and playing back the calls on less-than-adequate speakers diminished the fidelity of the actual calls.

In some cases, I was able to distinguish the voices of the crows played back at home on my computer. I made recordings of a similar call in all three of the crows' voices and electronically spliced them onto one track. Played back-to-back, it was possible to hear a subtle difference in timbre between their voices, although it would be difficult to pick out this slight variation of tone without the aid and luxury of listening to these calls repeatedly on a recording. It was an exercise in details; careful study could give an edge when listening to crow voices in the field. I include the spectrogram here of this recording. It can also be heard on the Web site CawOfTheWild.com.

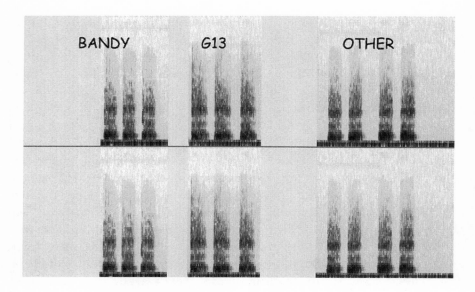

The more I played these calls for the crows over the course of time, the quicker they were to dismiss and ignore them as trickery or false alarms. Even Bandy soon became disinterested, as though realizing a real crow did not make the sounds. Had he lost interest because the machine did not respond as a real crow would have? G13 showed me that she understood where the sounds were coming from by looking directly at the device from which they emanated. Perhaps being around people had taught her that they sometimes operated machines capable of producing sounds. Perhaps she was even astute enough to observe the other sounds my computer made as I turned it on and had surmised that I caused the cawing with my noisy box.

G13 had her own unique call, which I never heard the other two birds imitate. It was probably a natural crow sound and was identified in the literature as "woo-ah" notes. The call was reminiscent of the song of joy Willy had sung to me at the park. G13's own twist on the call sounded much like a human's sharp intake of breath followed by a high, sweet wooooo, that sometimes rose slightly on the final elongated syllable. I came to know this as a friendly sound; the sweet lilting tone most likely reflected its intent. I let G13 know that I liked this call by talking to her when she produced it, and as a result, she used it even more to please me. I could usually induce her to make the call by imitating it myself, and, in fact, it became a ritual we shared, a way I could interact with her from the other side of the bars. The tone she used when making this call and her desire to please people best summed up her personality.

All the crows at one time or another sounded off to announce the arrival of visitors. This was analogous to the Scrap family's habit back home, announcing my arrival from work. Whether a known staff member or a complete stranger had strolled in to look around, the cawing was usually the same. Categorized as an attention call, I believe it meant, "Look! Someone is coming down the walk." Almost without exception, one of the crows greeted every visitor in this way. Whether they took turns at this duty and why it was important, I cannot say for sure.

Occasionally the crows sounded alarm calls. It was not always apparent what they were reacting to, but it was easy to hear that they were indeed frightened of something. Once a work crew cutting down a large tree across the street caused the alarm. This work also made the crows huddle together on the main tree perch, acting like black statues. It may have been unfamiliar sights and sounds causing their fear. Perhaps because trees are such an integral part of crows' lives, seeing one destroyed scared them at an even deeper level.

Once I dropped a blue jay feather into their cage to test for a reaction, and all three crows began to scream the agitated and frightened, "Kek, kek, kek." Perhaps they associated the feather with the torn remains left by their enemy the hawk. Might they be his next victims?

The captive crows also exchanged contact calls with the wild crows in the area. At times, Bandy and G13 seemed to be calling a duet, each taking a part of the same message. Bandy favored the high staccato machine gun sounds, and G13 sang raspy, drawn-out notes. Listening to these calls from a distance along the trail behind the center, I pondered possible reasons for this duality. If I were a crow who could not see the two callers, it would still be clear to me that there were two crows talking. Might they be telling me that they were a mated pair? Would a larger group of crows calling together adapt a different register or a different call to delineate their numbers?

The third category of calls I heard from the captives was the most intriguing. Reserved for intimates, these vocalizations were too quiet to be heard from a distance. This category included G13's woo calls, Bandy and Other's signature boings, and a low "Aaaawk." The one soft sound significant by its absence was the rattle I so often heard among the family groups around home. Since I'd always felt this was an aggressive/possessive call, it appeared there were no aggressive challengers among this group, at least not during the times I observed them.

Without the choices or family ties that would have been available to them in the wild, these crows had no choice but to forge relationships. I had heard rumors that two other crows living with these crows had died mysteriously. Ben said that autopsies had been preformed, and, save for liver problems in one bird, no disease process had been identified. This left their demise open to speculation. Some staff members postulated that the surviving crows were aggressive and had killed the other crows. I dismissed this theory as unfair, as from what I had heard, there had been no marks on the dead birds. The theory seemed based on the notion that crows are mean and evil, and that they are always viciously killing each other.

I watched the caged birds carefully for interactions that might tell me how they felt about each other. I noticed that two of the birds seemed to pair off, spending time perching together on the main tree. It appeared that Other and Bandy had formed a bond of sorts. When the two crows sat together quietly, I could sense an extreme intensity between them. They seemed to tune into each other during these times as though communicating in some way humans do not yet understand. At times, Bandy would fluff his head feathers while gently touching Other's bill. Other would flash her nictitating membranes, allowing this interaction, but then suddenly swipe at Bandy with her beak, ending Bandy's advance. Other seemed conflicted or ambivalent toward Bandy. I wondered how G13 fit into the equation.

I got a partial answer to my question on a sunny day in June. Bandy, as though on impulse, flew over to join Other, who had been resting on the main tree perch. He sat right next to her. G13, who had been watching intently, reacted immediately by jumping to the main tree also, keeping two to three feet between her and the other birds. Bandy and Other both signaled with their nictitating membranes, as though in a state of high emotion. Bandy opened his beak in an exaggerated gape then slammed it shut with a clack. This gesture seemed threatening to me, but judging by the ensuing events, it was clearly not. The pair engaged in billing. Bandy lightly touched Other's cheek and slid it along the side of her face and beak. This also seemed to be an emotionally charged event for G13. She watched them intently. While Other and Bandy rested in low crouching positions, Bandy engaged in strange statues behavior—at times with his beak open. After about ten minutes, G13 began to quiver her tail. Was this motion a sexual invitation to Bandy? Was she trying to lure him away from Other? Just as quickly as he had approached, Bandy flew away and began preening. His actions induced G13 to begin preening also.

While this scenario made me think that Bandy had a sort of crush on Other, it appeared to be somewhat unrequited. Other most times was a loner. G13 and Bandy interacted most frequently. One day after a bath in the water dish, G13 and Bandy sat together on the main perch. G13was sleepy and tucked her head into her wing to doze. Bandy, in a very playful way poked, at G13's head. It was plain to see that it was all a lighthearted game. G13 woke briefly but then, still sleepy, tucked her head back into her wing. Bandy then began to pull at G13's beak, nudging her to stay awake. For a moment I became alarmed because G13 had such a glazed-over look. Was she sick? I have since learned that hers was the normal behavior of a very sleepy crow. The interaction reminded me of two siblings goofing around and teasing each other. While certain future events would lead me to believe that G13 had designs on Bandy, he appeared to think of her as a kid sister.

Over the course of the year, I noted many instances when G13 would usurp Other from a perch. She would either land near Other and then displace her with her whole body, or she would land on the perch below Other and snap or bite at Other's feet. Other almost never reacted with aggression and moved quickly in deference to G13. Only once did Other beak swipe at G13. But the fit of temper was short-lived. Other did not show fear but rather acceptance of her place in the scheme of things. Perhaps she even understood the reason for G13's actions—she was jealous of the attention Other received from Bandy.

This one-sided rivalry cast Bandy in the role of peacemaker. He clearly did not intend to ruffle G13's feathers and even appeared to make efforts to appease her agitation. An interesting exchange illustrated that my suspicions were correct. I was about to leave for the day, but I stopped to visit with G13 near the high box. I wanted to observe the inside of her mouth, as it was a warm day, and both she and Bandy had their beaks open. Bandy was on the eagle perch, and Other was poking around on the ground, eating. All at once, Other approached Bandy with her head bowed forward and her neck bent. At first Bandy gently and tentatively touched Other's cheek and beak with his. He then gripped Other's beak, clacking his own over it a few times—a gesture that seemed playful. He next opened Other's beak and scooped out a bit of food. Was it the equivalent of crow kiss? I was extremely surprised that Other had approached Bandy. It was the first time I had witnessed Other initiate any contact toward human or bird. Within seconds of this encounter, G13, who had been watching intently, jumped down and landed next to Bandy. Bandy immediately made the boing call and then moved away from both of them, as if to diffuse the situation. G13 and Other squared off and spent the next few minutes continuously beak wiping their respective perches. Clearly, there was some intense emotion between the two, necessitating the displacement of aggression with this gesture.

Within the next five minutes, Other became animated, jumping about the cage with her head fluffed and finally bathing in the black water dish several times. She seemed to be having a nice time cooling off this way. It was amusing to watch as she dipped her head beak first into the water while flashing her nicti-tating membranes and then splashed herself silly. When she was done with her several baths, she retreated to the high part of the main tree and began aggres-sively hammering at it with her beak. Perhaps she needed to vent a little pent up emotion after her encounters with Bandy and G13.

I observed no instances of overt aggression between the three crows. Any momentary annoyance was just that, a swipe of the beak or a toe bite, and then on with business as usual. In general, the tone in the enclosure was amiable. The captives seemed to think of themselves as a unified group of sorts, evidenced by the fact that all three often gathered on the very top of the main tree for rest. Their calls also served to unify them; many times all three answered the wild crows or joined in calling an alarm.

The wild crows in the surrounding forest were an important source of social communication for the three caged crows. These groups regularly conversed with each other. A few times, I was able to follow the context of the interaction. Once I came upon the group in a high state of agitation. All three captives were sound-ing excited alarm calls, joining in with several wild crows in the area. The wild crows were circling above us in the air, and I looked around carefully for anything that could be causing the disturbance. High, high above us, soaring on a wind thermal was a hawk. This example seemed to illustrate that the three caged birds felt a part of the larger group of crows in the area, and participated in a hawk alert just as if they would have had they been free.

Once, on an extremely cold January day, I came for my visit dressed in a hooded down jacket and big black mittens, carrying a black camera bag. The crows didn't recognize me right away, and the sight of the black bag and mittens sent them into a panic. Even removing my hood and talking to my pal G13 did not immediately calm the group. Their hysteria brought in many crows from the neighborhood, and they circled over me, cawing, ready to mob the unknown danger. G13 gripped a branch of the main tree and began flapping her wings. It made her appear very infantile. I wondered if this "fear flapping" was a form of begging or an attempt to look like a juvenile so as not to be attacked by the terri-fying intruder. Fearing this loud cacophony would draw the staff, I placed my black mittens and camera bag out of sight. Still, crows screamed above my head until by talking softly I was able to break the spell. G13 calmed down, and once she realized it was only I, she seemed a little sheepish to have called out the troops. The neighborhood crows dispersed as suddenly as they had appeared. It appeared that the wild crows also considered these jailbirds part of the larger group. Later, upon seeing my glove on the ground, G13 approached and cawed a message directly to the evil black thing. It sounded less like fear than a reprimand for causing her such alarm.

I often wondered exactly what the wild crows made of this arrangement, if they realized that the three crows were not free to travel as they were. In January, to the time of year crows begin thinking of pairing off, a wild crow landed above the cage on a branch. He began a warbling cooing serenade, sounding like the Pavarotti of crows. Other and Bandy all but ignored him, but G13 reacted by quivering her tail and body. Was it possible the wild crow had come to court, and G13 was responding? Did the wild crow realize the futility of his intentions?

In general, Bandy seemed most interested in his wild friends. He often sat with one eye pointed skyward, scanning for activity and calling, "Come here," repeatedly should any crows appear. This activity led to the need for "spy holes," in the black tarp covering the cage wires. I had observed Other tearing a small hole in the heavy cloth and then pressing her eye to the opening, checking the regions of the world previously obscured to her. Bandy also made use of her handiwork, and he sometimes dashed to a spy hole to follow a wild crow across the sky.

I once witnessed a conversation between the two groups that sounded suspiciously like each caller was enunciating the call or pattern for the sake of clarity. It was not unlike talking through a bad phone connection. Each speaker seemed to press to make sure the other understood. The caws were distinct and chopped off at the ends, with long pauses between. "No," they seemed to say, "I said, caw...caw...caw...caw...caw." The exchange held another secret from the mysterious world of crows, and while I could share the experience, I could not understand it.

Food was another important focus of the captive group. Bandy seemed obsessed at times with rearranging his caches. He spent the most time of the three engaged in this behavior. There was an ample supply of food at all times for all three crows. But all three still felt the instinctive need to cache favored bits for later. Perhaps they did it to fill the empty hours, but most likely they did it because it's what crows do. G13 and Other didn't seem to take it too seriously, but Bandy made it into his job. He became particularly annoyed if either of the other two birds tried to steal his caches or disturbed him while he was "working."

I once witnessed Bandy cache a piece of meat. A short while later, G13 uncached it—presumably to eat it. Her action brought Bandy swiftly down to the ground, where he swiped at her with his sword like beak. Stealing and coveting went on with items other than food as well. I observed all three crows, at one time or another, caching small twigs. Once when Other was playing with a stick,

G13 pursued her, interested. When Other dropped the precious item, G13 quickly pounced on it, grabbing the stick and caching it in almost one motion. It was hard to imagine a use for this behavior in the lives of these crows, if not as diversion from boredom or simple jealousy over another's possession.

Some days when the crows were not engaged in any interesting activities, I would look for ways to liven things up. G13 and Bandy would often look on inquisitively as I stood behind their high box and pushed up objects they had wedged between the bars of the cage and the wooden back of the box. Using my pen, I could loosen the forgotten treasures and make them once again accessible to the crows. Other watched from the main tree, but G13 nosed her way face-to-face with me as I freed bits of twigs, small pebbles, or fragments of chicken bone once tucked there for safekeeping. Bandy peered over G13's shoulder, and she always allowed him to have first choice if he wanted to grab an item. She cooed her friendly greeting to both of us as we played.

This game gave me the idea of picking a dandelion leaf from the weed patch at my feet and handing it to G13. Since she was less afraid of me and stood closest, Bandy was not able to grab this novelty. I thought the crows might appreciate a familiar item from their former environment, and that the leaf would impart a bit of energy into an otherwise dead space. Save for the other crows, all the items they came in contact with were dead and devoid of the lush green of the surrounding forest. The inside of their cage felt as barren as winter even in the midst of summer.

The dandelion leaf was a big hit. G13 immediately absconded with it to the main perch, Bandy at her heels. How excited she was with this prize as she fingered it with her beak repeatedly. Bandy quickly made a stab at grabbing it from her, missing once, before finally engaging in a tug of war that broke the stem in two. Not satisfied, he threw the piece he had won to the ground and grabbed the other half from G13. Neither of the birds rescued the torn pieces from the sand, and it appeared the object of the endeavor was possession rather than actual interest in eating the leaf or using it in some way.

I witnessed crow logic at work as G13 played with a leaf in the large black water container. She was carefully trying to place it over bits of meat that lay sodden in the dish. Was she trying to use the leaf to cache these foods, or was she just playing in the water like a child? This activity drew Bandy's interest, and he came near to watch and then pulled his own leaf through the cage bars. He abandoned his own leaf shortly thereafter and chose instead to steal G13's leaf, experimenting with it in the same way she had. Was it through their natural curiosity and their manipulation of the environment that wild crows discovered useful things that help them adapt?

Stories abound of crows dropping nuts from high perches to crack them, but Bandy used his environment to hull a nut in a different way. Apparently not fond of the thin skin between the shell and the peanut, Bandy invented a useful system for the efficient removal of the offending cover. He would carefully wedge the nut between his perch and the side of the metal cage. With the nut immobilized there, he could easily work away the thin membrane and get to the peanut. While not exactly tool use, this process is a clear example of using insight to solve a niggling problem.

At other times, the crows' insight seemed a bit misguided. One of the staff used a purple Frisbee as a training tool. If the crows produced the behavior she was looking for, the reward was mealworms. The Frisbee acted as a bridge letting the crows know they were heading in the right direction. She would show it to them as visual positive reinforcement for any correct attempt, intermittently feeding them mealworms from the disc. Eventually, the crows associated the purple Frisbee with a favorite food. One afternoon as I came upon the crows, Cheryl had just finished cleaning the cage and had inadvertently left the Frisbee behind. After she locked up, and I was alone watching the three, both Other and Bandy approached the purple disc that was now lying on the low box. They took turns hammering at it, as though expecting their action would produce mealworms. They looked under the disc and then began producing behaviors they thought might make the Frisbee give up the worms. Bandy placed both feet squarely on the disc and made several of his signature boing calls. It seemed that the crows had no idea that a person was needed to provide the worms and believed that this magical object could produce them if only they could discover the hidden key to unlocking its power.

While this incident does not illustrate that crows are geniuses, it does show that they are willing to experiment with and manipulate their environment. Creativity and curiosity are the hallmarks of intelligent creatures. A willingness to try new things may lead to a discovery of the useful sort.

The crows' intelligence on certain days led to mischief. While standing at my usual post, I heard Cheryl's dismayed muttering near the kestrel cage. She was scanning the ground in the crow cage, and when I asked her if she had lost something she said she had in fact accidentally dropped her key in the crows' cage earlier. Just as I was about to say that I hoped one of the crows hadn't snatched up the shiny object, we both saw that it was in fact true. That little imp Bandy had made off with it and was now picking it up and dropping it on the high box, listening to the noise it made—no doubt enjoying his new toy. Just as I thought he might, Bandy played with the key for a few more seconds before caching his treasure in the sand below. I glued my eye to the spot in the sand, while Cheryl ran off in search of a spare key. Although I never moved an eyelash, it was harder for two humans to uncover the key in the sand than it would have been for Bandy alone. Without a doubt, he would have gone right to the spot without a moment's hesitation.

I had witnessed countless examples of these captive birds retrieving cached items in the sand where I could see no visible marker. I had also seen them digging and swiping in the sand where they thought something should be and coming up empty. It was certainly more than luck at work when they did find hidden food. I also wondered how many of their misses were due to the fact that the sand was raked every day, removing some of the scraps of food and disturbing any markers the crows may be using to remember their spots. Bandy and G13 favored certain areas to cache and hunt for food. G13 liked to store hers near the fence in the doorway area, while Bandy went through the extra bother of climbing high on the cage wire above his favorite perch, and caching between the roof and the top portion of the cage. I often thought he cached there to better guard his loot, since he spent so much time on that particular perch anyway. This was a likely strategy, since these crows were never above stealing from each other, and in fact paid extra attention when others were caching food.

Recent research conducted on a beach in Washington state indicates that the sentinel behavior exhibited by what researchers had assumed was an altruistic member of the flock might very well be scouting by a larcenist noting his comrades' cache sights for future retrieval. It was previously believed that crows posted guards to watch for predators while members of the flock were feeding. But researchers James and Renee Ha watched for thousands of hours while crows stole food from each other. Some birds they banded and observed were honest and never stole from each other, preferring instead to find their own food supplies. Other crows' food sources, however, contained up to 65 percent swiped merchandise. Pushing their conclusions even further, they tried to find DNA links between the birds to test whether crows steal from their own relatives. If the early conclusions from this research are correct, not only can crows recognize close relatives, but they are less likely to steal from them as well.

That crows steal from each other's caches did not come as a big surprise to me. I did wonder if local or familial custom played a role in how much or little crows pilfered from each other. With a creature as complex as the crow, it would not surprise me to find behaviors and mores unique to certain areas or groups as opposed to global truths about crows' stealing from cache sites.

I was perplexed by Bandy's behavior one day when I offered the birds a small chunk of chicken I had saved from my dinner. There was only one piece, and Bandy grabbed it first. He apparently did not care to eat it immediately, and after hopping about with it, he unburied a nut and shoved the chicken into its place, leaving the peanut on the surface of the sand. He then retired to his favorite perch. What was he thinking? My first impression was that he was offering a trade to the other two birds, knowing that he could never escape their watchful eyes. By leaving the nut exposed, perhaps he was inviting the others to take it in exchange for leaving the chicken he had just procured. Maybe he remembered where he cached things by using a limited number of spots within a certain area, cutting down on the number of places he would have to remember and making it more likely he could recover all of his caches. Perhaps he had usurped the peanut because all of his spots had been filled. After a few moments, when neither of the other birds took the nut, Bandy returned to it and cached it in a different spot. Had he withdrawn the offer of a trade, or was this behavior without purpose? I never knew.

My own relationship with these crows became more intimate as the days passed. They clearly recognized me, and I believe they expected my weekly visits. G13 became my favorite, as she was unabashed in her affection. She showed uncommon interest in any conversation I might have with a passing human, alighting on the closest branch and listening intently. When we were alone, she developed a curious habit of biting on a small protrusion of twig on one of the perches nearest my post. Whether motivated by a nervous habit, boredom, or another mysterious purpose, she repeated this activity numerous times. An accumulation of saliva would form as she worked her tongue on the small twig. Sometimes she would flap her wings as she chewed. I wondered if her display was directed at me.

Bandy had lived up to his name on more than one occasion. Once, as I tried to identify the birds before continuing my notes, I noticed the bird I thought was Bandy had a green ring on his leg. I had already identified G13 by her signature wing flicks, but it was only when the third bird rose up off of his perch that I realized that all three were now sporting the green bracelets! This change would certainly leave me at a disadvantage for quick identification, but the center was less concerned about my identification technique than they were with state regulations. All captive birds must wear a leg band. My Bandy was no exception. As I was digesting this new twist, Bandy flew directly toward me and landed with a *thunk* on the bars squarely in front of my face. Bandy wasn't one to approach me in this way. If he acknowledged me overtly at all, it was only to respond to my dropping nuts into the cage for him, and then he only eyed me carefully. As he leaned over to pick at his new bracelet, I was able to see that a part of the number read "49." The coincidence stunned me. I had been concerned with getting a closer look at the number on his band so that I could confirm my observations of the birds in the future. I wondered if he could have somehow understood my intentions. It wasn't the first time I had felt as though a crow had read my mind. Had Bandy understood somehow what it was I sought, or was he merely showing me what they had done to him since I had last seen him? Perhaps was even asking me to help him remove the offending nuisance.

It was difficult for me to escape detection at the nature center, standing around observing the crows week after week—especially when using my video recorder. It was only a matter of time before one member of the staff or another wandered outside to do something, and we struck up a conversation. First Ben and I renewed our acquaintance, and little by little, word slipped out about what I was doing. The staff began to offer valuable bits of information that gave me a fuller picture of the events at the center. When I found out that Kathleen had quit shortly after I left, I became more comfortable there, and after a cold day shifting from foot to foot in the snow, I began visiting inside as well.

Once I was inside, the sounds of Jo Jo and Ollie calling from the second floor always lured me up to say hello. Fragile and scruffy, Ollie would make his small mewing sound as my fingers tried to reach his neck through the metal chicken wire for a scratch. Jo Jo was easily engaged, and I took to bringing her small treats from my lunch, which the staff allowed me to feed her. She pounded chicken bones with relish and delicately fingered the small bits of roast beef with her beak before swallowing them. Her eyes lit with delight as soon as she saw my hand reach into my pocket. Ollie was harder to accommodate, as his loss of vision caused him to snap his beak randomly in the air at the offer of a treat. More times than not, he missed out on these snacks as they fell into the pile of muck at the bottom of the cage.

One day Janet was kind enough to open Ollie's cage to allow me to pet him. Unlike the first time—and no longer encumbered by the duties of cage clean-ing—I was able to concentrate fully on petting him. It requires a great deal of coordination and control to pet a bird, as their light weight offers little resistance to pressure. It is almost like trying to pet the air. Ollie's deteriorated condition only exaggerated this effect. He reminded me somehow of an aged Chihuahua. I petted him for several minutes, as Jo Jo grew restless in the cage next door. Janet admonished Jo for being so mean and told her that if she were nicer she could receive this treatment also. I was continually surprised that people working with animals and birds could be so ignorant of their ways. It seemed obvious that this crow was not inherently mean but handicapped by the detriment of living in such limited circumstances. Her response to the environment was governed by fear and a lack of socialization toward her captors. But by far, the most important ingredient missing from her life was love.

On a subsequent visit I thought about how Jo Jo greeted me with her signature, "Hello, hello," and then stuck her beak through the cage bar and waited. Preconditioned by the employees' prejudice about her temperament, I at first thought her greeting was a trick to get me to put my finger near so she could bite it. The red sign above her cage warned in big letters, "I bite." But that day, my curiosity got the best of me, and I raised my plastic pen and tapped her beak cautiously. She did not make any move to snap at the pen but instead blinked her nictitating membrane in approval. I petted her a few moments in this way and thus began a ritual that continues to this day. She allowed me to scratch her head and neck with the pen, falling into a sleep-like trance so deep that it took her a few moments to recover. Here I had found a gentle, loving bird hiding underneath a distorted image forced upon her by her keepers. It was apparent to me that somewhere in her past a person had loved her dearly, and she had never forgotten, despite the desolate stretch of time that had become her life. Eventually I became brave enough to substitute my vulnerable finger for the pen. Jo Jo solicited this attention from me whenever I visited, first rewarding me with her talking trick and then presenting her beak and waiting patiently.

I taught Jo Jo a simple trick using an empty cat food can. Capitalizing on the joy she feels when pounding with her beak, I began tapping out the first part of the rhythm, "Shave and a haircut," and coaxing her to finish with "two bits." She picked up the concept almost immediately. I was not surprised by her ability to rapidly assimilate new information, but I was intrigued by an incident that occurred as a direct result of this new game. Once as we were playing, she accidentally missed the can and almost pecked my hand. She froze in place, and I could easily read her body language. She appeared stricken by her mistake, embarrassed and sorrowful at having unintentionally crossed the lines of friendship. I could see that she did not want me to read ill intent into this act. Her eyes widened; she became still for a moment. "Oops," her actions seemed to say.

I became an advocate for the crows. I spent time fixing their perches and enriching their enclosures, once by dragging a discarded Christmas tree into their outdoor cage. With the staffs' consent, I worked at making soft perches for Jo Jo's burgeoning foot ailments. With my head and arms inside her cage, while Jo Jo lumbered back and forth like a drunken bear, I wrapped the branches she used as perches. Her level of trust for me was much higher than mine for her. I had a respectful fear of the pain she could inflict on me, should she choose to. But she never chose to do anything but try to get in the middle of the action, much like a cat who insisted on getting under the sheets when someone was trying to make the bed.

Jo Jo did help me once in this endeavor. I had found that the thick, scratchy burlap wrap that Kathleen had originally secured around the perch was soggy and laden with bacteria. I decided to remove it. It proved a cantankerous task, however, as the knots on the rope holding the burlap in place stubbornly refused to surrender to my fingers. Jo Jo, as usual, watched my movements closely. Finally acquiescing to the rope's greater power, I headed downstairs to retrieve a pair of scissors. Upon my return, I was stunned to find that Jo Jo had used her formidable beak to loosen the tie, not only correctly reading my intent, but also providing the brute force that I lacked. I had never questioned her intelligence, but I was amazed that she had figured out a way to help me.

13

Playing God: Don't Try This at Home

In my role as observer of crows, I began to see a more detailed picture of Riverside itself, one that had only been hinted at during my short tenure as a volunteer there. Many members of the staff became like friends, and I overheard conversations with callers to the center, as well as walk-in patrons who brought in an assortment of wildlife.

There was a disparity between the Riverside Nature Center visitors recalled from youth and Riverside as it exists today. While struggling to understand this incongruence, limited by the stories handed down the line by those who had passed through the doors as workers, I stumbled upon a book written by Miss Judy herself. There before me were the words, thoughts, and feelings of the legendary pioneer of the Riverside Nature Center. I would no longer hear her voice as interpreted by others.

What shone through her words most vividly was her deep love for animals. Her knowledge base was impressive, and I learned much reading her accounts of native species. She gave careful and detailed portraits of the animals she had come into contact with. Rabbits, flying squirrels, raccoons, salamanders, and a screech owl were among those who found their way onto the pages of her book. She strove to replicate the animals' natural environments and foods as closely as possible, providing live bugs gathered by the local schoolchildren and hollow logs as familiar homes.

In fact, it appeared that the local children figured prominently in the day-to-day maintenance of the center. They exchanged their labor for a chance to be near these creatures in this zoo without bars. Miss Judy allowed many of the creatures to have their run of the place, not requiring them to be caged. They were free to alight on visitors, to come to them for behind-the-ear scratches, or in some cases to nip at them when the mood struck. Miss Judy readily admitted to trying to convert these wild creatures into pets, and she described a view of wildlife that I interpreted as unrealistic. It was clear her heart was in the right place. But like the cat woman who takes on more cats than she could possibly care for, her beliefs led her into a gray area that bordered on animal abuse.

When we are young, or even in later years as an idyllic fantasy, we would all like to believe that Gentle Ben really exists. But if we work toward a selfless love and respect for wild creatures, we begin to understand that they are not pets meant to fill our empty hearts with their love and dependence, but regal creatures meant to enjoy the life nature gave them. This is not to say that rehabilitation sanctuaries have no place, as under the right circumstance, they can be an extremely valuable educational tool—not to mention a compassionate haven for otherwise doomed animals.

Miss Judy reigned for fifty years, right up until her death. She worked and lived at Riverside, devoting her energies to her cause. Certainly, cultural beliefs about wildlife changed significantly over that span. Where once we used animals indiscriminately in the circus and in other forms of entertainment, the modern focus has shifted to the conservation of their environment. While Miss Judy respected all living things, her methods were misguided, especially by today's standards. Her ideas about keeping wildlife without cages could only have meant that the center was filthy and dangerous. Current staff members familiar with her eccentricities share horror stories of rat infestation and sixty-five cats living in the basement. Judging by Miss Judy's own interpretation of events, I tend to believe the staff stories are based on fact rather than exaggeration. Perhaps Miss Judy fancied herself a modern day St. Francis of Assisi. Whatever distorted glass she saw through, the vision of what she hoped Riverside could be did not match what it actually was. Similarly, the current staff at the center had fallen short of an ideal that was both right in some ways and wrong in others.

I had to wonder how Miss Judy would feel about some of the things I saw at the current incarnation of the Riverside Nature Center. There was the time when a mother brought in her school-aged child, who tenderly grasped a shoebox. "What have you got there?" Deb inquired as they headed toward the center. It was a nest of fallen sparrows, barely old enough to identify. They shifted from foot to foot when Deb suggested placing them back near where they had fallen, so their mother could find them. It was a familiar phenomenon at the center that people came there to "save something," and wouldn't be happy until they had done so, even if that meant sacrificing good advice for glory. Sensing it was what they wanted, Deb directed them inside to the man at the desk, but she cautioned that he would probably tell them the same thing. The man at the desk that day was avid conservationist John Chelsea, not a lover of the interloper the non-native house sparrow.

We were surprised when the pair returned a few minutes later without the box, grinning from ear to ear. "The man at the desk knew exactly what they were, and he told us he would take care of them," the young girl beamed. Deb and I passed a knowing look between us. Sickness welled in the pit of my stomach. We knew what John meant when he used the phrase "take care of." To the saviors, it meant John would sit up all night, feeding the little ones with a toothpick dipped in dog food. But Deb knew that before she could race the distance to the lab, John would have dropped them in the plastic bucket, closed the lid tight, and turned the handle on the metal tank of CO_2 gas that would end their lives. Surely, Miss Judy would have wept at her fallen sparrows that day.

As I learned about the center's crows, my understanding of the life of a wildlife rehabber deepened, as did my ability to relate to the staff's gallows humor. I engaged in a bit of it myself from time to time, although I was acutely aware and ashamed of it. While visiting with the staff one Sunday, I came upon what I callously referred to in my head as "box o' birds." It was an open plastic box of dead birds all piled on top of one another. Too gruesome to be real, it reminded me of a grotesque scene from a film. A medium-sized brown bird was almost unrecognizable, although it was most likely a female or baby cardinal. A tiny common yellow throat lay straight legged in rigor mortis, the remnants of some makeshift splint visible around its leg. On the very top of the pile lay an all-black bird, its head concealed beneath it. It seemed too small to be a crow.

I stared at it for the longest time, trying to make out what it was. I wanted to touch it, but I still felt that I was not really a part of the center and that I had no right to poke around in its business. I began to think the bird was a baby crow. Finally, I worked up the nerve to ask Janet as she passed. I could never be sure if she heard exactly what I said, as she lived in a world made hazy by hearing loss. She relied partially on lip reading, and this process sometimes made it hard to enter the place where her true feelings lived. "I don't know," she shrugged at my question, displaying her characteristic mask that said she did not care too much. I guessed it was how one must become in order to continue working there.

Eventually, Deb turned the bird over for me, and it became obvious that it was in fact a crow. It was probably a youngster culled from the group or fallen from the nest prematurely. It looked surprisingly old, but I supposed even a baby could look aged in death. Its head was pulled into its chest, as though it had tried to hide from its fate. Fully feathered, it still had the characteristic short tail of a young bird. Just to be sure, I asked Deb to open its mouth, and the baby pink confirmed it. Its pointy tongue did not fit my imaginings, since I had been using only the inside of my pet budgie's mouth as reference. I had never examined a crow's mouth so closely.

The constant barrage of failure and death are a part of every wildlife rehabber's life, Miss Judy's included. Birds piled in a plastic box are the logical symbol of how helpless we are to save the world. Whereas Miss Judy likely believed she could save the world, the current center crew is much too grounded in reality. The public expects these workers to provide answers that will sit well in a gnawing conscience, but they don't want any of the responsibility or the work themselves. The constant conflict between trying to appease the public yet tell the truth as they know it sometimes leaves rehabbers too raw to deal with the few who might learn from an honest yet compassionate response.

As the seasons changed, I began to piece together a coherent picture, of life at the center and life as a crow in a cage. Visitors, even the many who commented that they were "just crows," might have expressed pity for the poor birds locked away in misery. But I concluded that the three had compensated for their lack of freedom by refusing to give up on life. They made the best of the circumstance and continued to live the life of crows, socializing with each other and interacting with the world around them.

My questions about wildlife rehabilitation were not as easily dismissed. Some days I looked at the imperfect care animals received at the center and the circumstances for the injured populace as a whole, and I came away thinking it would be a blessing if the director had his wish. The remaining residents would be lost to attrition, the aging structure surrendered to static displays, and John Chelsea freed from the burden of its living sculptures. But then I recalled my first visit to the upstairs nature room and the awe I had felt at being closer to the creatures I could only admire from a distance. Perhaps there were others like me who came away inspired from the experience. Did it matter if those numbers were smaller than the troops of disrespectful children who screamed at the birds and poked at them through the bars, or the adults who were out for a Sunday stroll and did not even see what they were looking at? If the Riverside Nature Center did not exist, I believe society would lose another small piece of its humanity. For it is not whether we fail at the task but that we have the heart to set out and try it in the first place. Riverside's contribution to wildlife, and to humankind, lies in its efforts to reach for a higher vision. My hopes lie in the future, which I want to believe contains a better, more modern version of Miss Judy—one whose passion for wildlife is not crippled by distortion or jaded by hardship and failure. I want to live in a world where we care deeply about all of our inhabitants, where we provide refuge and help to those we have injured. It would be a colder journey indeed without at least the illusion of such caring, without those who endeavor to mend the broken and set them right again. As long as humans are filled with compassion, there will be a need for sanctuaries such as this.

PART III
Summer 2002

14

CT's Surprise

It was time to file income taxes, and this chore was on my mind as I walked through the courtyard of an office complex during my daily work. I heard a strange birdcall, like a duck, but my keen ear told me it was Corvid. I followed the sound to a medium-sized evergreen tree. Could it have been the location of a crow's nest? It was much too early in the year for a young crow to be begging. But that was what the sound reminded me of—sort of plaintive "Baaaa, baaaa," almost like a helpless lamb bleating. I stood underneath the tree and looked up to see a crow perched above me on a branch. I checked carefully for a nest, looking for signs of what I knew would be a large bulky platform of sticks. The tree was thick with evergreen boughs, and I strained to make out any indication of what was causing this crow to soliloquize. But it was merely a lone crow singing an odd song.

Approximately forty minutes later and several miles away, I heard a similar call in the distance, which led me to believe it was a seasonal practice. Most likely, I had witnessed a female advertising at a potential nest site. Female birds often mimic fledgling young during breeding season and are thus fed by their male partners.

At home, the Scraps were using the birdbath to soak grape-like berries, returning for them later, after they were reconstituted. I knew they had to have been at work on this year's nest; maybe they were even tending a clutch of eggs, waiting for them as they waited for the berries. A female cardinal was fussing with some sticks in the large evergreen shrub in front of the house. Just as I had deduced that her behavior might mean young birds or eggs, so did a member of the Scrap family, who sat quietly in the maple tree. Perhaps Mrs. Cardinal would soon decide it was not the ideal spot to raise a family.

CT Parker had been strangely absent from the park of late, and the signs that my predictable world was crumbling disturbed me. I had come to expect the crows' strange behavior this time of year, but I somehow hadn't expected it from

CT. Was it possible that my young bird was preoccupied with a nest? He was only two years old, younger than the average breeder, according to McGowan.

I heard a crow sound off in the distance, and, thinking it might have been the wayward CT, I rushed over to the park. There were several crows picking through the garbage next to the maintenance garage. They scattered at my approach, but I found they were acquaintances of Willy, who stayed behind, running to greet me with his signature wobble. He took several nuts and flew off toward his own section of the park, just as one of the Scraps arrived to escort him over the boundary line, should he have forgotten his manners. I walked over to his area, where we visited awhile, two old friends sharing a snack. I reflected on how long he had known me, still remembering our bond even after his family had carried him to unknown parts. I wondered if he ever reminisced about his visits to my garden, as I did or if he sometimes spied me from a distance and recollected me fondly. "Where is CT?" I asked him, as if he could answer.

Would it be May if I did not spot the tailless Wilbur? I saw him one day as I was driving down a busy street a few blocks from home. He was perched atop a light post, and I tried to get his attention through the windshield as I passed. I don't know if he recognized my car or me, but he did fluff himself and shake at my passing. In my parakeet this was a sign of acknowledgement, if I walked into a room and spoke to him he would fluff and shake in this same way. I was glad to know Wilbur was ok, and wondered idly if he parked himself there waiting to catch a glimpse of me.

In late May, Willy made several forays into his parents' old territory. Once, upon seeing my car pull out of the garage, he flew toward me, hoping to catch my attention. Just as I was rummaging around in my pockets and thinking of pulling over to see him, the Scrap crows drove him off. Of late, the Scraps had begun using the spaces the W's had formerly used, not confining themselves to just eating off the roof. They cached their food in the same section of the park reserved for Wilbur and Winona and visited their section of the railroad tracks, parallel with the maple tree. The old W territory had become a free-for-all, it seemed. Willy visited the area once again, startling me by how closely he landed at my feet. He seemed to appear out of nowhere. I only got a brief look at him before he was shooed away by the Scraps.

On the very last day of May that year, CT Parker resurfaced. After wandering around the park waiting for crows and finding none, I gave up, turning to go home. Suddenly I had an urge to look behind me, and there he was. It was uncanny the way I sensed his presence, and I wondered about the connections between all living things—the unseen threads that link us with our loved ones.

CT immediately came to me, and I spoke to him of his long absence. He looked just fine and flashed his nictitating membrane at me in response to my words. He seemed a bit nervous, possibly due to some young girls playing nearby, and he left rather abruptly. Willy appeared then, circling over my head, but he only landed long enough to grab a nut before taking off.

Shortly thereafter, I notice that there had been a shift in the other crows' attitude towards CT. An unidentified crow tried to attack him one day as we visited in the park. It surprised us both, and CT flattened himself to the ground so hard and fast that he fell to his side with an audible "thwack." The other crow then chased him, as CT tried to shake him with the "crash crow" maneuver. One of CT's allies, whom I didn't recognize, came to his defense and began cawing angrily. He wiped his beak vigorously on a tree branch and also pulled at small twigs to further show his displeasure. This crow continued to caw intermittently in an urgent manner, and CT was able to return to me and collect a few nuts. Acting fearful of another broadside, he cast his eye skyward while listening intently to the cawing in the distance.

I witnessed a similar incident about two weeks later, only this time I was able to identify the other parties involved. Willy and another crow—whom I assumed was Willy's mate—started a fight with CT. Again, CT's partner demonstrated great frustration by picking at twigs and dropping them to the ground. The bird was angry, whereas CT just tried to avoid the confrontation. It surprised me that Willy would act with such pointed aggression toward his young offspring. What factors would have caused such behavior? Was it possible Willy was aware that CT was tending a nest? CT certainly wasn't helping with Willy's nest.

Meanwhile, near the grove of trees on my work route, where I had heard the strange calls of a crow earlier that spring, I now heard the sound of a young crow. I counted three babies above me on what looked to be their first adventure. One was looking bewildered and crying for his parent to come back, but another was more curious about me. He returned my gaze without fear, and I could sense that I could tame him as easily as Waif or CT. A few trees over, there was a very young crow, napping next to his parent, who eyed me carefully but decided against alarming her brood. There was probably a nest hidden somewhere nearby that had eluded me on my repeated passes through this area since my first encounter with the singing crow, some two months before.

Early on the morning of the Fourth of July—before the fireworks fans in my neighborhood had arisen after their premature celebration of the previous night—I walked slowly through the park area near where CT hung out. I was starting to piece together some theories based on the events of the preceding weeks. I had begun to suspect that CT had taken a mate, as a certain crow would often be with him who began taking nuts from me after following his lead. She would stay farther back, and once or twice she had appeared without him, keeping his territory and watching me from above. She usually attracted Willy's attention, and he would try to drive her off—and vice versa. CT's large father did not intimidate this plucky crow, and the anger he caused her gave her an edgy verve. Was it possible that the two-year-old CT was already breeding? Had my misfit crow found his match? If so, his mate was the complement of the gentle, placid CT, and perhaps it had been her idea to pair up with him, picking him out of a group of birds whose tails were perfectly straight. Judging by his loyalty toward me, he was most likely a devoted mate with keen pair-bonding abilities. Still, I couldn't be sure my ideas were anything more than speculation and the projections of my feelings toward my favorite member of the Parker family.

Then came the day I knew for sure. My suspicions and half-realized glimpses from the corner of my eye came to fruition. I turned the corner of the park maintenance garage and surprised four crows who had been feeding on the ground. One crow startled and began a series of hysterical alarm calls. Two of the other crows followed her to the safety of the high branches, but the fourth, whom I quickly recognized as CT, approached me. By now, the cloud in my head was diffusing, and I realized finally that the alarmed bird was Mrs. CT, and she was directing two baby crows. My CT had had a successful nest that year. I had been right about the crow I believed to be his mate, and now here was the proof—two freshly fledged young crows.

His mate's continued screams caused CT to behave erratically. He seemed torn between the life he knew and the friend he had known to be safe, and his responsibility to his mate and offspring. One of the babies refused to heed his mother's warning and instead followed CT in taking nuts from me. The baby did not appear to know what to do with them, but the curiosity that would help him to survive in this world had gotten the best of him. He cocked his head to one side to give the nut his full attention. He had the clumsy charm of any young creature. Mrs. CT continued to shout intermittent alarms, while CT landed directly above my head on a low branch. He became very calm and still, as if to tell his mate I was not dangerous. During the short time I had known her, she had begun to trust me, but having her young charges so near me was too much for her to accept.

Both crows would agree to teach their young to fear humans, but I was the exception to the rule, and the parents were in conflict as to how to explain to them. Mrs. CT preferred to tell the children that all humans should be feared, while CT, swayed by his experiences and the nuts, was torn. In the mysterious way of crows, this conflict was resolved by the next day. It was mid-morning when I set out to look for the newest branch of the Parker family. I passed the spot where CT usually met me, and it wasn't until I got all the way to the far end of the park, where the woodpeckers drum the trees, that I heard the first sign of crows in the vicinity. It was Mrs. CT, calling a mild alarm. I heard the babies answering from the trees off to the right. She was less fearful of me than she had been the day before and allowed me to approach her babies without shouting in terror. I tossed a nut in their direction, and CT appeared out of nowhere, trailed by the younger of the two babies, whom I called Indy, in honor of meeting her on the Fourth of July. After observing CT eating the nut, she began her plaintive begging. Because of his calmness and comfort level with me, I was able to observe this behavior from a mere eight feet away.

I doubted many people had seen wild crow families at this distance, and a deep feeling of privilege overwhelmed me. CT was still feeding Indy occasionally, but he was also trying to teach the youngster independence, and he displayed his irritation at her begging. He swiped at her with his beak a few times but mostly ignored her pleas, continuing to work on the nuts himself. He tried to show her by example what to do, but she preferred the easy life she had known in the nest to this confusing world. Indy showed her frustration by quivering her wings and gaped with her wide red mouth. She rarely tried to eat the nuts on her own, but a few times she picked up a crumb and was successful at getting it into her mouth and swallowing it.

The other baby descended from the tree. She was quieter, less frustrated, and more inquisitive. I named this bird Liberty. She seemed to take the lessons of nut eating more seriously, picking up the empty shells to study. She copied her father's hammering motions with her beak. When tired of this new game, she wandered off on her own, attacking a bug on the bark of a tree, practicing a lesson she had already learned. Born first, she seemed eons ahead of her sibling.

Both of the youngsters knew how to caw in answer to Mrs. CT's alarms, and they paid attention to calls in the distance, answering in kind. Mrs. CT stayed perched in the tree the whole time, possibly to keep a better eye on things, while CT pouched large quantities of the nuts for later. He spit the lot out and ate a few, before re-pouching them and flying off toward the tracks. Although still mesmerized by the scene, I realized our visit was ending and reluctantly tore myself away. Before heading home, I left a pile of nuts for the reticent Mrs. She waited until I was a safe distance away before gathering them up. As she soared past me, with Indy and Liberty close behind, I heard Indy's impatient squall.

As I walked home, I wondered what factors could explain CT's early reproduction. Could he have taken up with a more experienced female who had lost her first mate? Could the area support many crows and, if so, would such a circumstance encourage early breeding? Were there other intrinsic factors that humans cannot understand about the choices crows make?

Two days after I met the latest crow family, Willy announced the birth of two more progeny. This fact did not surprise me, but I was bowled over to find that CT was tagging along with his father, mother, and the two new fledges. I considered that I might have misinterpreted Indy and Liberty's lineage. Could CT have been babysitting for Willy? And for what reason had the aggression between the two dissipated, allowing CT to join this group? Careful watching over the next few days, I learn that both Willy and CT have had young this year, when I see both families foraging in the park at the same time.

Near the month's end, however, Willy once again resumed dive-bombing CT when he saw him in the park. It was another unsolved crow mystery. Could the presence of CT's mate have had an effect on Willy? Could CT's status as a breeding crow have caused Willy to try to drive him away?

Accepting my limitations at interpreting the crows' actions, I instead enjoy Willy's new children. He proudly leads his family toward me, two gawky black forms, with his mate bringing up the rear. It was the first year Willy's mate had shown any interest in me, and she had become quite friendly toward me and my pocket full of peanuts. I decided to call her Clever Girl and hoped I would have the chance to get to know her better. It appeared the two had split up the duties of teaching, each taking charge of one of the offspring. The fledglings were sticking close to their appointed parent, watching everything.

I was waiting patiently for the return of the W's, and I watched with interest for any sign of the Scrap family's new brood. The Scraps were certainly keeping any successes from their clutch well hidden. But a young bird's curiosity could only be contained for so long, and the newest Scrap crow made his debut in a rather dramatic fashion. Attracted by the honking sound of a juvenile crow, I looked up from my deck chair just in time to see a wayward bird streaking across the sky. It was obvious to me that he had escaped in a direction that his older guardians did not intend, and they chased him, shouting admonitions.

My impression was that the adults had not wanted this newly fledged bird to fly off on his own, especially in this direction. They followed helplessly, eventually landing next to the baby in Winona's tree. I imagined that the baby had watched the activities of this area from a distance and finally made his break to see firsthand what went on in the yard and on the roof. I studied him with my binoculars as he studied me. It seemed to me the world was bursting with young crows, and I was glad for it.

The baby then flew to the park, and the entire Scrap family followed him there. The cat was out of the bag now, and they probably figured the only recourse was to keep a close eye out for danger and otherwise let the little one find his way. All at once they began to call out in fear and perched themselves atop the fence near the baseball diamond. These alarm calls attracted Willy, and he flew over to see what the fuss was about. I flew over too, and found the source of the commotion: a small black plastic bag.

Leaving the Scraps to their neurotic fears, Willy and I returned to his area of the park so I could monitor the progress of his family. One of his offspring was beginning to understand the value of a peanut, swiping the pieces that Willy dropped, while his sibling stayed farther back with Clever Girl. But in the wink of an eye, the Scraps became upset, driving Willy away and insisting I only feed them from my endless supply of nuts.

On my way home I spotted two crows perched on the light post on the far side of the railroad tracks. I suspected that it was the W's, surveying the scene for their eminent return. In fact, the next day Wilbur triumphantly met me at my regular dog-walking time, and I whispered my jubilant greetings as he perched above me. "We're back," his eyes seemed to tell me. Just then, I heard a honking sound overhead and in that instant—almost mistaking him for a goose—I named Wilbur's latest creation. I broke with tradition and called him "Honk," since it fit him and his distinctive voice so well. "Have you raised him with a brood of geese?" I asked Wilbur. Honk was a demanding little bird, following Wilbur relentlessly and grabbing without regard to manners at any scrap of food within reach. He reminded me of Waif at that age, and I spotted Winona looking on with a weary attitude that told me I was right.

Each year when the W's returned I was filled with the gratitude of the undeserving. So many things in life disappeared, sifting through our fingers, furnishing the material of our darkest nightmares. But the universe had returned to me the birds I loved, again and again, so that I could savor the delicious warmth of an empty vessel filled. The W's were back, and the full richness of summer could begin.

15

A Murder of Crows

With the return of the W's I fastened my seatbelt as I waited for the yearly territory struggles to take place. If I had learned one thing in the time I spent watching these birds it was that they were unpredictable. Why for example had the W's returned so late with their new brood? It was mid-August, a full month after their usual return. Had they conceded the battle of the roof to the Scraps? Did it have anything to do with the drought conditions in the area?

They were certainly enthusiastic about seeing me again, warming immediately to our old friendship. "We can only meet you at the park," Wilbur seemed to say as he buzzed my head at dog-walking time.

As I reoriented myself to the W family, I was surprised to learn that a third adult crow was traveling with them. He obviously knew me, so I surmised it was either Wally or W4 from the previous nest. Wilbur and Winona had only produced one new bird from this year's clutch. Is this why the extra crow had returned with them?

It was after only a few days of our park visits that unsettling events began puzzling me. The Scraps, current holders of the rights to the roof, became sporadic visitors in the mornings. Maybe they were acquiescing to the W's this year, I reasoned. But the W's were not quick to fill in the void. In fact, only Winona and Honk had been meeting me in the park lately. It wasn't like Wilbur to miss a day.

I spent some time at the far end of the park looking for CT. Only one unidentified member of the Parker family was present. The crow flew toward me for some nuts, but picked at them listlessly, cracking them open but not eating them.

One of these facts contemplated singly would not be worrisome, but stacked together they were starting to build a frightening picture. Why were so many of the crows missing at one time? I shook my head with the frustration I always felt at the mysterious ways of crows. I sometimes felt the harder I studied them, the less I knew of them.

I caught glimpses of the Scrap family, as they furtively flitted through the trees and that gave me hope that things would soon return to normal. But I couldn't imagine why the Scraps were not taking food from me anymore.

When I noticed that there were only two out of the seven members of the Scraps hanging around, I began to get alarmed. But when I saw that the adult of that pair was acting ill, I became panicky. She sat on the peak of a roof in the fluffed posture of a sick bird. The younger bird with her seemed disoriented and nervous, as though without guidance, he did not know how to behave in his environment.

I watched them obsessively. By now, they seemed to be the only two crows in the area. I tried tempting them to land on the roof with extra special treats. Small chunks of steak, and a crab leg were noticed, but left untouched. I tried hard to woo these crows. The adult crow seemed to be responding to me. She watched where I went, and what I did. Once, as I glanced over my shoulder in her direction I saw her leaning low to avoid a visual obstruction to see me better.

Maybe I was wrong, and she wasn't sick. The absence of her family and neighbors still troubled me though. Could it be that population fluctuations, or environmental changes had caused the other crows to frequent more attractive areas? Still I couldn't shake the feeling that the attention she paid to me had a desperate air, as though I were a port in a storm.

We both perked up when we heard some distant caws coming from the direction of the W's territory. She took off in a flash, calling with excitement. She was not defending a territory it seemed, but rather, rushing to greet her own kind. I was glad.

The joy was short-lived when confirmation of my suspicion of her illness came the very next day. In the park, heartened to see a crow on the ground in the Scrap's territory, I raced to get a better look. Something wasn't right. This crow was standing in the middle of a mud puddle with a glazed look in her eye. As I approached, she scarcely moved. I knew instantly that the bird was gravely ill.

I wanted desperately to help. I walked right up to her, and was almost within reach of grabbing her. But I would have to think this through. What would I do if I caught her? I couldn't take her to Riverside Nature Center. I didn't trust their help. I began talking to her. I didn't care if bystanders could hear me anymore, this was a desperate situation. "Come home with me, and I'll try to help you," I beseeched. As I coaxed, she began to follow me like an imprinted gosling. What was I letting myself in for?

I relived the dilemma of that first injured sparrow, the catalyst for my stint at the rehab center. Nothing mattered anymore except my crow. But in that moment, she took the decision from my hands. She stopped following me, and began to flee. I did not pursue her aggressively, because I didn't want to stress an already sick bird. I followed her slowly, still talking to her. She made it clear that she would not let me catch her, as she flew to the low branch of a tree across the street from my house.

Like a child wiggling a loose tooth, I checked and re-checked her status in the tree. She sat unresponsive, like a stone. Her eyes stared blankly ahead, but she did not see. She did not seem connected to this world anymore. I repeated this trek until darkness made it hard to find her, and I reluctantly retired to my bed for fitful sleep.

In the morning, she was gone. I knew she was dead. I had witnessed enough sick birds at Riverside to know that. Had she met the end in the talons of a hawk? Or had she fallen from the tree when her spirit finally released her earthly form?

Her younger companion stayed in the area for a few days. He darted around the neighborhood acting skittish and confused. The young crow had no one to teach him. Would the food I provided on the roof be enough to help him survive? I would be no substitute for the extended family of crows he was missing. I witnessed him hanging around with a flock of sparrows, scrounging the scraps of bread they had found. I could not coax him with my peanuts. This lone crow cawed every morning from the park, but no one answered him. Then he too became silent and disappeared.

The day was muggy and hot, but a chill settled on my insides. There was a silence, despite the chirping sparrows and the late-summer cicadas, the motorcycle speeding by and the children's excited voices from the pool across the way. It was silent for a sound I longed to hear. Not even one crow cawed in my neighborhood that day. Missing were the alarm calls, the young fledglings voices in the trees, and the casual, "Caw, caw? Are you near?" The air conditioner's rattling hum accompanied the pond's lonely splash. I heard my tears fall above the rustle of the trees. No one seemed to notice the gaping hole in the natural world as they hurried by, their lives going on as usual. But life had changed for me in a way I could never have anticipated.

I stared at the food melting on the garage roof, leaving a stain on the green gritty paper; I stared at the empty telephone wires. The nuts on the roof had been banished by the wind to the gutter. For a desperate moment, I contemplated the world without crows.

When the Scraps stopped coming to eat in the morning, and the other crows in the area disappeared without so much as a molted feather left behind as a good-bye note, I tried anxiously to dismiss my fears, but reality is a persistent stalker. I consoled myself, but the comfort was hollow.

I searched for Willy, CT, and the Parkers and longed to see the W's, who had only so recently returned with Honk. Their absence was ominous, and it pierced the veil of false bravado I had tried to hide behind.

Religiously, I walked to the park, scouring land and air for signs of crows. I searched for a round white stain under a favorite perch or a molted feather in a telling place. Each day, I became more frantic, picking up and inspecting promising feathers, only to concede that they were too brown to belong to a crow. I called up the memories of the last few times I had seen the crows, as though these thoughts were treasured jewels to be examined again and again. I replayed the scene of tossing Honk a nut on the baseball field and turning to see Winona looking on with interest to see what the newest member of the family would do. Honk was a fast learner. Having only met me the day before, he had already decided that nuts were good to eat, and I was trustworthy. He took the nut and began to crack it. I left several more for Winona and watched as she gathered them and flew off to the railroad tracks. I thought it odd that Wilbur had not returned with her that day, but I did not realize that what seemed an insignificant event would mark the last time I would ever see my first family of crows.

I supposed a lot, trying hard to fit unsettling circumstance into a neat and tidy bundle. Maybe, I conjectured, the crows had changed their foraging patterns due to the extremely dry stretch of weather. But every one of my rationalizations was accompanied by a sinking feeling. Witnessing the death of the crow at the park was the card that trumped all speculation. Something was just not right, and I thought I knew what it was. I had heard about it in the news, and I had felt it lurking. It was the monster called West Nile virus.

The virus, transmitted by mosquitoes, first appeared in my state in 2001. The crow was its most susceptible victim. For reasons unknown, they, along with other Corvids, are most vulnerable to its wrath. Fatality in crows infected with the virus is believed to be near 100 percent. This was dismal news. When I heard of the virus, I thought of it as I thought of any other peril a crow might face. Keenly aware of the mathematical probability that I would outlive my crows, I expected losses. In fact, I had already faced them every time the babies of one year decided it was time to move on. But to lose all of the crows in every one of my family groups was inconceivable. But that is what appeared to have happened.

My heels hurt from my many impromptu forays into the park, my feet clad only in soft-soled moccasins. Finding even one living crow became an obsession that gripped me each waking moment. My walks became restless searches ending in despair. I began to have auditory hallucinations of crows cawing in the distance, but the crows themselves never appeared. I realized it was just the madness of my grief. Would I ever see Wilbur and Winona again? Would my last memory of Willy be the pride with which he had led his family at our last encounter? Would I never again see him happily running toward me, reminding me of the enduring loyalty of the American crow?

As I passed the trashcans near the park maintenance garage, visions of CT haunted me. I recalled his first silly moments out of the nest and his willingness to take nuts from a stranger. I could see his awkward, puny young body—brownish and weak—perched on the fence, where he sat and listened to me to talk on his first day in his new world. Then I saw him as he had appeared just a few short weeks ago, a beautiful, glossy specimen—albeit with a crooked appendage—carefully monitoring his new fledglings and taking orders from his bossy wife. My most engaging CT, I still couldn't believe he could be gone. Would I forever be expecting him to appear as I passed his special spots?

As time passed my speculation about alternatives to West Nile diminished, and it became painfully impossible to believe that anything but the virus had taken my crows. My tears gave way to anger. A wound opened inside me, letting in dark, self-pitying thoughts. Why had my crows been taken from me? It had been the one part of my world I foolishly thought I could control. These crows were not people who would abandon and hurt me. These crows were not pets who would eventually die before me. These crows were a legacy of love from the skies. Generation upon generation was introduced to me, and we had carried out a healing communion. The young crows had learned their love of me from their parents, who had gladly taught them of my existence. I thought this gift would last forever. But I was wrong. In many ways, I had defined myself by my ability to tame a wild crow. I had worn it like a special badge. Not many people could claim what I had achieved. I wasn't just another speck, living a life of conformity.

My anger led me to wonder who—if anyone—was monitoring the crow population. Crows were hunted in my state with no limit to the number a shooter could take down. Was allowing such hunting foolish in light of what we knew of this crow-killing virus? I didn't know. Recent research has shown that it is possible for crows to pass the virus amongst themselves after a mosquito has infected one of them. The local Audubon society conducted an emergency crow count and concluded what I already knew. The crow population in the city and surrounding suburbs had been almost entirely wiped out. Places where large numbers of crows were expected yielded single digit numbers, and in some instances, that single digit number was zero.

As Sunday approached, the day I had reserved for my weekly visit to Riverside, I looked forward to seeing my captive crows. These were the only crows I had left in the world. Although my visits of late had become more habit than study, I still looked forward to seeing the familiar black forms. I felt I had learned what this group had to teach me, but they could still surprise me occasionally during the course of their daily routine. I wouldn't abandon my old friends simply because they were no longer useful.

It seemed years since my home crows had come to visit on the telephone line. Had it only been a few weeks since their inexplicable evaporation? I missed a crow's presence in my life. After four years of watching for crows, listening for their voices in the distance, and stretching my mind to understand their behavior, it was hard to believe that all I had now were captive birds limited to life in a sanctuary cage.

It was quiet as I walked up the path toward their enclosure, and I pushed a thought away. I scanned the main tree perch for Other or Bandy. I pushed the thought harder. I turned the curve of their enclosure and came to my usual post. The cage was stark and empty, like a hospital bed freshly made, sheet pulled tight. That damn virus had gotten them too! Without memory, without a body, I floated through the doors to the office. My right hand pressed my heart, as though to stop it from crumbling. The expressions on the faces of the staff told me what words could not.

Sounds became distant, people swirled, and my vision tunneled. There was one bird left, I was told—whisked into the center hospital after the other two dropped so suddenly. "Can I see him?" I voiced quickly. There in the lowest metal cage was a small crow, dishonored by the soiled papers and the lumps of dog chow on the floor. In this setting, it took a moment to recognize the crow, to understand whom I was to mourn. "The one with the big beak?" I asked Deb and Janet. It was Bandy, the errant feather on his right wing providing the final confirmation. He looked tiny, not the majestic peacekeeper he once was.

I began to cry as I knelt there by his cage. Not these birds too! I pulled myself together to get the details of what had happened. Other had died first, on Wednesday, I determined by their description—dropping suddenly without any warning. G13 died on Saturday morning. I recalled suddenly how she had not said her usual good-bye to me the Sunday before, and I wondered if she was already beginning to feel ill. It hardly mattered now, as nothing could turn the clock back to a day when she lived.

The sudden demise of his two companions had left Bandy bewildered and agitated. Whether crows are aware of death or grieve the loss of dead comrades is open to debate, however anecdotal stories of crow funerals abound. Regular bird-watchers as well as casual observers report ritualistic proceedings coinciding with the appearance of dead crows. The birds gather from far and near, as though to pay last respects to the fallen, sometimes observing an eerie silence before departing. Several years earlier, I had witnessed what I at first believed was a crow funeral. Awakened at 5:00 a.m. by the cawing of many crows, I had scrambled outside to see what had my group so agitated. Above me, twenty or more crows flew in a circle, cawing a steady beat. As I reached the hub of their circle, I saw a black form lying still in the street. I saw what I thought was a beak pointing skyward. Attempting to absorb the scene and its meaning, I crept closer, trepidation rising at which of my friends had lost its life. When my eyes could finally focus clearly, I saw that the broken black thing was not a crow but a cat, its lifeless ear pointing skyward. Had the crows gathered to see their diminished enemy, or had they been fooled like me by the illusion the cat presented?

Bandy was still with us, but nothing could ever be the same. The three cage mates had broken up for good. My mind flashed to the sound of their thuds as they landed on the wooden boxes and scratched across the sandy surfaces. Bandy's fate was uncertain, since he had most likely been exposed to the virus himself. Deb passed me an article confirming that although we don't know exactly how, crows can pass the virus to each other if the mosquito infects one of them.

I spent some time on my knees visiting with Bandy. He did not seem himself, but how could he in this tiny metal hospital cage, after losing the two crows with whom he had spent all his time. I was sad when I left him, not knowing if it might be the last time that I ever saw him alive. As I departed, I made Deb promise to call me right away should he die. I needed to know as surely as if he had been a relative or my own pet.

That night as I sat on the deck the world seemed more hushed than it had been, even in the past week of waiting and hoping my suspicions were untrue. I thought of the crow I had heard cawing in my dream early Saturday morning, and I wondered if it had been G13, saying good-bye as her spirit flew past. The silence had taken on a new tenor; it was no longer just the absence of caws but also an absence of the spirit of the crows themselves.

With trepidation, I visited Riverside the following Sunday. I held my breath and braced for bad news as I opened the heavy wooden door. After all, Deb might not have kept her promise to call. I was greeted by the raucous reverberating call of a crow cooped up in a metal enclosure. I felt like cawing myself.

Bandy hopped back and forth between the scraps of tree branch placed in his cage. I knelt and talked with him in tones reserved for someone who had just beaten certain death. It had been several weeks now since the disease had attacked his friends, and since the incubation period is from three to fourteen days, I could almost breathe a sigh of relief. I heard a voice behind me, "Are you afraid of worms?" "No," I lied as the hand belonging to the voice passed a gritty clump of cold mealworms to my palm. They begin to wriggle as they warm in my hand. I hold one squirming victim toward Bandy's beak. He won't take it directly from me, so I drop it through the bars. He snaps it up immediately swallowing it quickly live. I rejoice at seeing his ravenous appetite.

Later Deb confided that even though Bandy had passed one hurdle, his life could still be in jeopardy. I was saddened but not shocked to hear that John might order him put to sleep even if he survived. John felt strongly that a crow should not live a solitary life. I was not an objective observer, but I felt that putting Bandy to death would be wrong. I weakly justified his life by appealing to John's biologist side: Bandy had survived West Nile virus and so must have had antibodies that could be valuable to scientists studying the disease.

The sick feeling I had about the possibility that my friend Bandy's life would be unceremoniously snuffed in the bottom of a plastic bucket was deflected by the humorous and twisted plots we concocted for spiriting the poor bird away. It was such gallows laughter that allowed me to keep thinking and not shut my mind to the brutality of Riverside. I was aware for the first time that I was becoming what I had so fought against becoming. I laughed in the face of death, because doing otherwise would render me incapable of moving forward, of keeping my eyes open to the truth. Someone called out from the front line, "Do we know who takes baby chickens?" "Dominick's Finer Foods," I quipped callously. As I joked, another part of my soul and mind still reflected on the grim realities and searched desperately for solutions.

I considered what options may have been best for Bandy, feeling a responsibility for this life that we as humans had taken control over. Perhaps he could be released if the only other option was the gas chamber. His worst fate then would be dying in the peaceful green of the surrounding forest. He had a slim chance of surviving on his own. If he were released into the wild, could I trust Riverside to do so in a professional way and not just open the window and say, "Shoo?" Bandy would almost certainly run into trouble if they took this cavalier approach. Local crows might not be willing to accept him into their family groups, and he could be ostracized, or worse. Would he know how to forage for natural foods after cage life? Could he truly fly long distances, gain altitude, and manage the rigors a wild life would require? I felt it best that he live out his life in captivity. After all, he had entertained us all these years, posing for our snapshots and acting as a living picture book for our small children. We owed him that much. I believed the humans who had once helped him had now handicapped him and should therefore provide for his needs.

Deb suggested staging an escape, but feared that if she were on duty she would become suspect. Since she had opposed John with her outspoken suggestions, she might become a likely focus of blame. My plots were leaning in a more Machiavellian direction. I thought we should save the next crow body that came in and slip Bandy's green band onto the leg of the lifeless corpse. I was trying to work out the steps after that. I would have loved to have Bandy as a pet and would have cared for him until the day he died. However, the legalities of keeping a native crow, not to mention the guilt of having stolen him, helped me to restrain these impulses. And besides, we didn't know for sure yet what John's plans for Bandy were. The best I could offer now was hand wringing and serious thought. I would also contact anyone whom I thought could help.

When I got home, I wrote a few emails to local birders who had become pen pals of sorts due to our common interests. Most wrote back suggesting I kidnap Bandy. Perhaps I had secretly hoped that one of them would advocate where I had failed. Had I been a bystander aware of the situation and not a friend who wanted to maintain good relations with the staff at Riverside, I might have filed a complaint with the department of conservation or informed John's boss of his inclinations. But I did not want to implicate the sources I had within the center or cause trouble for them with John. So I just made others aware of the situation, worried, and decided to see what the next week would bring.

In the ensuing week, I heard about but missed a small feature on the local news showing Riverside and interviewing one of the staff members about West Nile virus. My curiosity was piqued as I made my pilgrimage to check on Bandy. What was the inside scoop on the visit from Channel 4 News? The front desk was unmanned as I entered, so I headed upstairs to see what Jo Jo and Ollie could tell me. Here I found Janet working on a snake cage, the long black reptile wrapped around her shoulders like a stole. I stroked the snake's body, amazed that something that felt so cool was a living creature. Immediately Janet told me that Bandy's life had been spared. I was elated at the news but surprised that a decision had been made, since John was out on vacation.

Deb appeared as Janet was putting the snake back in his enclosure. She filled in details of the news story. It seemed the request to visit had caused quite a stir, and an alarm call was sent out that brought the director of conservation over to act as a spokesperson for the center. The staff had not known what the director's visit was about, and it sent them into a panic. The cameras filmed for a half hour, but they had ultimately used only a tiny snippet of tape and a short statement from the spokesperson about the impact West Nile virus had had on the sanctuary birds. My intuition was flashing a red light. I had inferred that something said during that past week had saved Bandy life. I may never know if the information I circulated among my birding friends had made its way to the right ear, but whatever had happened, Bandy's life had been spared.

Janet unlocked Ollie's cage to pet and caress him, jokingly chiding Deb about not "appreciating the crows." Just last week, however, Janet had spoken nonchalantly about putting Bandy down. Perhaps Channel 4 News, acting on a tip, had gone snooping around the center for more than just a few quotes on West Nile virus. Perhaps their visit had made John feel that his actions were no longer taking place under the cover of darkness, that someone was shining a light on his base of operations. Perhaps other bird lovers had been disturbed by the thought of terminating the life of the resident crow.

Sweeping my speculations to the corner of my over-active imagination, I headed downstairs to see Bandy. He had many toys in his cage, some of which he found interesting and others, like the stuffed animal, he completely ignored. He liked the small plastic cup, and I floated it in his water dish like a boat. I mocked him in a teasing way, pretending to disturb his toys for the purpose of annoying him. He seemed to read my intent correctly. He made a frustrated "Aaaawk" at me and wiped his bill on the cage bar. He was not making a serious threat, I was certain. We invented a game together using small paper strips. I folded them over his cage bars, again feigning that I was doing it to bother him. I stepped away and waited for his response. He swiped at each one with an exaggerated flourish, ripping them off of the bars and tossing them to the ground. I continued this cycle with him, replacing the papers he had removed with my own exaggerated movements, mine more verbal than physical. He removed each strip of paper, sometimes placing them out of my reach and sometimes trying to cache them under the papers covering the floor of his cage. He was clearly playing along with the joke. Rather than just shoving the strips underneath the paper, he placed them there carefully and then tried to fold them by standing on them. He seemed to have the general idea of folding, but lacked the physical weight to complete the task. I wondered if I could show him how to make a crease by running my finger over the paper sharply. Could he do it, or would he only mimic this behavior with his beak?

This close proximity to Bandy opened up for me a new door to understanding his thinking, and I had renewed motivation to come back and visit him. Besides, it was downright fun to play with him. I was amazed at how quickly he had picked up the concept of our game and how rapidly he understood the subtext of my teasing. He had become a touchstone in my otherwise crowless world.

Over the next few months, as Bandy and I waited for the threat of the mosquito to dissipate, I introduced him to a new toy. A wooden call used by hunters for a more nefarious purpose might provide me with a way to interact with Bandy in his own language. I mustered my best imitation of a caw and waited for his reaction. He was interested but unimpressed by my silliness. Next, I tried calling to him from outside the open window, where he couldn't see me. He made it clear that he knew I was a pale imitation of a real crow, answering me with the same exasperated "Aaaawk" he used to humor me with while we played together.

I had come to understand the meaning of this sound as I had never been able to understand another crow call. I was convinced that Bandy used this particular call only to communicate with me. He even began to call in this way as soon as he saw me, as though calling my name. "You jester," he seemed to chuckle, as he waited for me with fluffed head feathers. I smiled at the thought of having made a crow laugh.

My resignation did not come easily as weeks and then months passed with no sign of my wild crows. The neighborhood felt empty. I forged an uneasy peace with the silence. I stared at the telephone wires and conjured visions of days gone by. I could almost see them above me, like clothespins on a line. But I was limited to my imagination, and I realized just how unique the experience of the last few years had been. It all seemed a dream now, memory melding with my sleeping visions of crows returning to me, reaching out with wings that became like hands reaching to comfort me in my grief. I prayed there would be cawing in heaven on the day I died.

I still walked the paths of my memories, looking above, listening for the wingbeats I knew would never come. And in my pocket, I fingered the cache of nuts waiting there.

Sources

Balda, Russell P., Alan B. Bond, and Alan C. Kamil. 2003. Social complexity and transitive inference in Corvids. *Animal Behavior. 65:479-487.*

Bentzen, P, et al. 2003. Kinship and Association in Social Foraging Northwestern Crows. *Bird Behavior. 15:65-75.*

Boyce, Nell. 14 Oct. 2002. Feathered Friends. *U.S. News & World Report.* 68–69.

Caccamise, Donald F., et al. 1997. Roosting behavior and group territoriality in American Crows. *The Auk. 114:628-637.*

Caffrey, Carolee. 2000. Correlates Of Reproductive Success In Cooperatively Breeding Western American Crows. *The Condor. 102:333-341.*

Clark, Robert G., Paul C. James, and Jeffery B. Morari. 1991. Sexing Adult and Yearling Crows by External Measurements and Discriminant Analysis. *Journal of Field Ornithology. 62: 132-138.*

Cornwall, D R., and G W. Cornwall.1971. Selected Vocalizations of the Common Crow. *The Auk. 88: 613-634.*

Goodwin, Derek. *Crows of the World.* Ithaca, New York: Cornell University Press, 1971.

Gorenzel, W. P., and T. P. Salmon. 1995. Characteristics of American crow urban roosts in California. *Journal of Wildlife Management 59: 638-645.*

Grout, Daniel J., Richard L. Knight, and Stanley A. Temple. 1987. Nest-Defense Behavior Of The American Crow In Urban And Rural Areas. *The Condor.89: 175-177.*

Heinrich, Bernd. *Mind of the Raven.* New York: Cliff Street Books, 1999.

———. *Ravens in Winter.* New York: Vintage Books, 1989.

Kilham, Lawrence. *The American Crow and the Common Raven.* College Station, Texas Texas A & M University Press, 1989.

McGowan, Kevin J. 2001. Chapter 17: Demographic and behavioral comparisons of suburban and rural American Crows. *Avian Ecology and Conservation in an Urbanizing World.* Ed. R Bowman, R Donelly, and J M. Marzluff. 365–381.

————. 1996. Family Lives of the Uncommon American Crow. *Cornell Plantations 51:1-4.*.

Moore, Jefferey E., and Paul V. Switzer. 1998. Preroosting aggregations in the American crow, Corvus Brachyrhynchos. *Can. J. Zool. 76:508-512.*

Savage, Candace. *Bird Brains.* San Francisco: Sierra Club Books, 1997.

Young, Andrew D. 1989. Body Composition and Diet of Breeding Female Common Crows. *The Condor. 91: 671-674.*

Web Sites of Interest

Crowbusters.com

Lodestone.org/people/hoss/ar/crowshoot/

CawOftheWild.com

978-0-595-36268-4
0-595-36268-0

6094953R0

Made in the USA
Lexington, KY
16 July 2010